COMMON SENSE RELIGION

*A Guide for Renewing Your
Christian Values*

GERALD MANN

MCCRACKEN PRESS
NEW YORK

McCracken Press™

An imprint of Multi Media Communicators, Inc.

575 Madison Avenue, Suite 1006
New York, NY 10022

Published in 1989 by Harper & Row, Publishers, Inc. and simultaneously in Canada by Fitzhenry & Whites as *Common Sense Christianity.*

McCracken Press™ is a trademark of Multi Media Communicators, Inc.

Library of Congress Cataloging-in-Publication Data:
Mann, Gerald.
  Common sense religion: renewing your
Christian values / Gerald Mann.
     p.   cm.
  Originally published: San Francisco: Harper & Row,
c1989. Includes bibliographical references.
  ISBN 1-56977-566-4: $8.95
  1. Apologetics. 2. Christine life. I. Title.
[BT1102.M293 1994]   94-27348
239—dc20   CIP

10 9 8 7 6 5 4 3 2 1

Printed in the United States of America

For Cindy
Who spoke courage out of her silence

For Stacey
Who spoke joy out of her laughter

For J. J.
Who spoke wisdom out of his cradle

For Lois
Who spoke life out of her grace

CONTENTS

INTRODUCTION

I have spent thirty years reaching unchurched believers and churched "unbelievers"—those who belong to God, but not to the traditional "box" that contains Him; those who belong to a church but not to the God preached by the church; those who want to give their hearts to God without losing their heads.

My sympathies lie with these people because I am one of them. I joined God early in life. I joined a church later. Then I spent years trying to squeeze the God I'd joined into the church I'd joined. After a while, I started trying to reverse the process.

Common Sense Religion is the best I can do to describe where I came out. I believe that the power we call "God" has made Himself known to us through senses which we all hold in common. As a Christian I believe that God's clearest revelation was in the person of Jesus of Nazareth who showed us both what God is like and what we are meant to become.

But Jesus never intended to start a new religion. Religion is what we humans have done to Christ. His purpose was to show us a way—a new way to do life—not to give us a body of doctrine, ritual, and structure. There is a place for such things. In fact, we cannot avoid them. But Jesus' way of doing life was founded on two principles: Love God as hard as you can, and love people as you love yourself.

"Love God—People—Self." Putting these words into practice has been our task for two thousand years. We've institutionalized them into intricate theologies. We've used them to wage bloody wars and justify political despots, and we've blessed a million souls with them.

We should never accept as final any interpretation or application of these words—even our own. All we can do is measure the way we do life by the way Jesus did it while He was among us.

You will detect that I am an exponent of the so-called "middle of the road." In Texas, we have a saying, "The middle of the road is for yellow stripes and dead armadillos—for cowards and confused varmints." I disagree. Yellow is the color of risk, the place for the unentrenched. The dead armadillos are the ones who catch it from the left and from the right. The middle is really the tightrope—the thin, shaky margin that hangs above made-up minds.

Jesus did life from the tightrope. He was taught by all and bought by none. The tightrope is the "narrow way" He spoke of. There's not much company there; few there are who follow it. But tightrope faith is the only way that leads to life in an uptight world.

Chapter 1

WHAT I KNOW I BELIEVE

I think I believe a lot of things. I'm sure I believe only five. I don't *know* that they are true. I probably couldn't demonstrate them to the satisfaction of everyone. But I'm sure I believe them and I know why. These are the five convictions I'm staking my life on:

First, I believe that God is out to make us all like Him. Or, to say the same thing another way, I believe that God is out to make us like Jesus Christ, who was both what God is like and what we're all becoming—Son of God, Son of Man; He answered to both names. He's what we're all coming to eventually. He is what God is going to make of the human race. He came to us backward out of the future.

How? And how long? However! And for as long as it takes! Either in this world or the next. Either in this history or beyond it. God won't give up.

Evolution makes sense. While everything dissipates and runs down, there's the countercurrent of developing life, this pushing upward from the lower to the higher. It's like the warm, life-laden Gulf Stream flowing up through the dark, dead, cold Atlantic.

The evolution of species is no threat to my faith. Considering how often I fall back into the slime, I'm not surprised to learn that may be where I came from!

Evolution is really a profound evidence of the propensity of God to create and make things grow. How easily we forget that what sets the God of the Bible off from the other gods is His absolute refusal to be static or fixed. He's a dynamic God who will not be located in anyone's particular idol, history, symbols, doctrines, or institutions. He's nomadic, constantly pulling things forward, constantly revealing more about Himself and us.

Our biological evolution is probably nearing its completion. Our spiritual evolution has only begun. We are just beginning to face the myths that divide people from each other: racism, nationalism, blood, creed, intellectual superiority.

In general, the human race is more civilized than it once was. In particular, of course, there are many exceptions.

But in spite of the "in particulars," there is at least one strong proof that we are moving forward: *We have learned to be afraid of ourselves.*

The key to human spiritual evolution is our capacity to be horrified by our capacity to do the horrible. After many wars, much carnage, and the atomic bomb, we now realize that we have the capacity—both technological and moral—to obliterate ourselves. The Russians may realize it more than we do. When we are afraid of ourselves, we are in the process of becoming more than ourselves.

Yes, God is out to make us like Him, that's the first thing I'm sure I believe. *The second is that each of us is either on God's Way or in God's Way.* We are either assets or liabilities to His purpose. We are either additions or subtractions.

In recent years, many Christians have jumped on the self–esteem–sloganeering bandwagon. We're told that we are "special" because we are creations of God and "God don't make no junk." I'm okay and you're okay simply because we *are.* In other words, we're special because we are conceived, come out of a womb, eat, drink, eliminate, copulate, procreate, and degenerate.

I have preached my fair share of that. But it's a half truth. We are special because we can contribute to what God is doing in the world. Self-esteem—the knowledge that I count for something—comes from counting for something. It's trendy to tell people how wonderful they are. It's true to tell them how wonderful they *can be.* Every person has a choice to be on God's Way or in God's Way: to add to the evolutionary process or subtract from it.

The third thing I believe is that *Whatever choice you make, it's gonna hurt.* Pain is endemic to life. The simplistic answer to Rabbi Kushner's *Why do Bad Things Happen to Good People?* is that bad things happen to *all* people! Life is a problem-solving venture.

I am amazed that we continue to be surprised by the bad things, that we dream of life without problems and are paralyzed by suffering. Lois, my wife of thirty-six years, and I were in the Caribbean for two weeks on a chartered sailboat. We did nothing but baste our bodies, talk, read, snorkel, look at the stars, and love each other. It was South Pacific, Camelot, and Lake Wobegon.

The day we returned from this paradise I had four nasty letters from television viewers, my dad was pronounced terminally ill, and I lost half my savings in a bad business deal. In the midst of my curses and wails my be-pimpled thirteen-year-old said, "Well, Dad, as you often tell me, 'Life's a zit and then you die.'"

As grotesque as it may sound, I believe that pain is actually a gift from God, and this leads me to the fourth thing I'm sure I believe: *Pain is always either the means to our end or the end of our means.* Either we use our pain to grow into the image of Christ, or we allow pain to paralyze us, freeze us in time, kill our growth.

We have been able to eliminate much physical discomfort through our marvelous technology. But many kinds of pain are nonphysical. In America, it seems that the relief of physical pain only intensifies the emotional, mental, and spiritual pain. And perhaps the worst pain of all is *ennui*— the emptiness that comes when we have nothing worthwhile to do or be.

Pain will always be with us in some form. To be human is to hurt. To be fully human—to be becoming, like Christ—is to use hurt as the stepping-stone. That's why the cross is the central symbol of the Christian faith. In order to live, He had to die. In order to live, we also have to die. We have to use our crosses, the ultimate one being death, in order to find life. The cross is the way to resurrection.

So what have I said? I'm sure I believe five things. *One:* God is out to turn us all into Himself. *Two:* I am either an asset or a liability. *Three:* Whichever I choose to be, it's gonna hurt. *Four:* Pain can either be the means to my end or the end of my means.

Number five is the most pivotal for me. It is this: *All of the above is garbage unless we've been grabbed by the grace of God.* I am unable to believe the four things I've stated without "outside help." Every conviction I hold can be shot down by at least a dozen sound arguments. Indeed, I can easily shoot them down myself.

The one thing that holds it all together for me is what I call God's grace, which has become a junk word in religious parlance. It now has to be defined by everyone who uses it.

For me, grace means guts—the guts to stand up and

take it. Grace is the guts to hold on—to a job that stinks, to a marriage that gets difficult, to a financial obligation I could "chapter eleven" out of, to a promise I could break, to an integrity I could compromise, to a commandment I could bend.

And grace is the guts to let go of what others are holding onto: my titles, ancestry, race, achievements, social class, and of course, my possessions. They tell me who I am. They set me off from others. My possessions are the grantors of my "face, space, and place." They are the means of measuring my worth as a person.

So grace is the guts to hold on and to let go; to hold on to what you cannot lose and to let go of what you cannot keep. That's what Jesus was talking about when He said, "For whoever would save life will lose it; and whoever loses his life for my sake and the gospel's will save it" (Mark 8:35).

He's talking about two kinds of life here: one that vanishes and one that lasts. Grace is the guts to hold onto the one that lasts and let go of the one that vanishes.

I believe that grace comes from God, but the question is how? Through what channels? There are many. Most are not mysterious and arcane. They are not of the "hovering buzzard" variety, where saints are overshadowed by a grace-mist while sequestered in their prayer closets. Much of God's grace comes to us unseen. For example, it comes to us genetically, through thousands of years of the "survival of the fittest." We are the heirs to millions of ancestors who stood up and held on, who have slogged through while the cowards fell by the way.

I'm not amazed at the number of people who fall apart and go crazy. I'm amazed at the number who hold together and go forward! Psychiatrists like M. Scott Peck are doing us a great service when they speak of human tenacity and resilience as evidences of God's grace.

I'm not astonished by how many people go out of this life kicking and screaming in terror. I'm astonished by the number who face death peacefully and courageously. (I once asked a judge in a small West Texas town how so many caring, honest, good folk could end up in such an ugly place. He said, "The weak ones couldn't take it and the sorry ones was all hanged or shot.")

God's grace also comes to us through such things as our immune system. At any given time, we have enough deadly critters floating around in us to kill an army. The healing process is still a mystery. We know that medicine is administered, attention is given, surgery is done, and some patients get well while others die.

We get God's grace from the tolerance and acceptance of people who love us. When O. J. Simpson was inducted into the National Football League's Hall of Fame, he spoke of his mother. After working as a hospital orderly in Los Angeles for thirty years, she took her first two-week vacation the summer of O. J.'s ninth year. The family traveled seven hundred miles to visit relatives. The third day after their arrival, O. J. was crying quietly.

His mom finally learned that he was about to miss his first Little League baseball game back in Los Angeles. She drove him seven hundred miles so he could play. That's grace.

One of my friends returned home from a speaking tour. His wife was washing his clothes and found lipstick on one of his shirts. "You must be careful," she said, "this stuff is really tough to wash out." Ministers get hugs from many people. Obviously she was aware of that, and this was her way of saying, "I trust you enough to assume that the lipstick got there in an innocent manner." That's grace.

God's grace, the guts to let go and hold on and go on, flows through countless unnoticed channels. Like water making its way to the sea, no mountain, wall, or desert can stop it. It will find a way to keep the cycle of life going.

But for me, these unnoticed channels are not enough to keep me believing. In fact, I lived for years without even seeing the grace of God in the things I've mentioned so far. I recognize these channels now for only one reason: I have been grabbed by the grace of God! God found me. I didn't find Him.

Anyone who has not had such an experience will find this strange. Those who've had it will say, "Yes, I know what he's talking about."

God's grace grabbed me when I committed my life to Jesus Christ. Like an eagle from the blue, God swooped down and picked me up. But how, when, and where it happened are not of primary importance. We get too caught up in describing the vehicle instead of what it carries. What carried me, what grabbed me, was "a knowing." I knew something I hadn't known before.

I knew that I was loved by God and always would be, without condition. There was nothing I could ever do to make Him love me more or less. And I also knew that He loved everyone else the same way.

It's knowing this that gives guts. It's forgetting it that gives grief.

This knowing, along with thirty years of falling down and getting up, of forgetting and remembering, form the linchpin of my existence.

I think I believe many things. I know I believe five.

Chapter 2

THE X-RATED TRUTH ABOUT GOD

Preachers should rate their sermons like the movies so that people will know what to expect. A G-rating would mean "generally acceptable to everyone." G-rated sermons are filled with such cream-of-wheat platitudes as, "Go ye into the world and smile." The congregation calls them "wonderful" or "marvelous."

GP-rated sermons are for more mature congregations. They mildly suggest change, but use big words and are subtle enough to allow the preacher to retract if he's challenged. These sermons elicit the response "deep" or "thought-provoking."

R-rated sermons mean "restricted to those who aren't upset by the truth." No big words here. The preacher tells it like it is. The preacher of R-rated sermons usually has an outside source of income. The congregation labels these sermons "disturbing" or "controversial."

X-rated sermons are absolutely limited to those who can tolerate having their minds renovated. They're the sermons that landed Jeremiah in the well and got Stephen stoned. They're called "shocking," "disgraceful," "totally unacceptable."

The truth about God's nature is X-rated. It's so out of synch with the human mindset that it's almost impossible to accept. Even those biblical heroes who were first given the scoop couldn't believe it. They kept second-guessing it and doubting its validity.

In the ancient tale of Adam and Eve in the Garden, it was Adam's and Eve's suspicion that God wasn't what He represented Himself to be that caused everything to fall apart. In so many words, the Serpent said, "God's doing a snow job on you. He doesn't want you to be free; He's not acting in your best interest." And they believed it. So do we.

When the religious leaders of Jesus' day criticized Him for hanging out with a bad crowd, He told them a story about a man who had two sons. One was a rebel who ran away and lost himself in self-destruction. The other was a robot who stayed home and lost himself in self-righteousness.

The father took them both back and made sons out of them. The father in the story is God. The sons are us. But we still have God all wrong.

Several years ago, I was asked to come up with a dramatic illustration of the X-rated truth about God for a conference of teenagers, most of whom were biblically illiterate. I made up a tale:

A hardened criminal is burglarizing a home in a quiet neighborhood. An eight-year-old girl comes home and surprises him. In a reflex action, he murders her. He's caught, tried, and executed.

Immediately after death, he finds himself in the proverbial dark tunnel being drawn toward a brilliant light. He emerges only to be received and embraced by his victim, the little girl!

He recoils, but he cannot resist. She leads him by the hand to the "Place of Re-experiencing." There he is made to see and feel two things. First, he sees the impact of his crime upon the girl's family and his own family. Second, he is enabled to see what would have been had he not committed his crimes. The girl was to have become a concert pianist, blessing the world with music that will never be heard. He himself was to have become a world leader!

Now he is taken to judgment. He is committed to serve for an indefinite time in a place called "LUA."

He pleads for punishment. God will not listen. When he arrives in LUA, he finds it crammed with people who fall into two camps: formerly violent folk like himself, both infamous and unknown villains, and religious folk who committed "velvet violence" against others. The "velvet violence" folks used threats and anger and scorn to manipulate and torture their victims into fearing a wrathful God. They made religion into an arid desert and God into a temperamental old crank.

All of the inhabitants of LUA follow the same regimen. Night and day they are loved by their former victims and taught about God's unconditional forgiveness. They constantly plead to be punished, but without result. There is only the love and forgiveness and laughter of God.

LUA stands for the "Land of Unaccepted Acceptance." All one must do to escape LUA is accept God's unconditional acceptance. But the story ends with our criminal begging for punishment, stuck in LUA.

What does the fable say? Hell is what we impose upon ourselves by refusing to accept God's acceptance of us.

We don't believe it because we keep trying to make God a larger image of ourselves. Because we don't love unconditionally, we refuse to allow Him to.

The outrageous truth about God is that He will love us all the way to heaven. We have no control over how He feels about us. We can't make Him love us more or less than He does already!

You want proof? Here's the proof. God went as far as He had to go to save us. And He sent His Son back to the very people who betrayed Him! That's what happened the first Easter.

Would you send your son back to the people who murdered him? I wouldn't!

Whoever heard of such nonsense! Shocking! Disgraceful! Totally unacceptable!

Did you say X-rated?

Chapter 3

THE LAST CHRISTIAN

George Bernard Shaw said Jesus was not the first Christian, He was the last one. From the crucifixion onward, the church has really not tried to be like Him.

For years I've heard cries for revival in the church, but I've come to suspect there may be nothing that admirable to revive! God doesn't live in the past, He lives in the future. (You can argue that He lives in the present, but it's already past with the saying of it. "Now" is a mere construction of mind and speech, a tool that enables us to think and talk. There is no "now.")

When the Bible says Jesus is the first and the last (alpha and omega), that's what it means. Jesus was the first human fully to do it God's way, and He was also the last. No one has caught up to Him since.

My point is that Jesus was the last human to be both the Son of God and the Son of Man. He was the last human to achieve at-one-ness with God.

People in His day didn't want Him to be divine. People today don't want Him to be human.

Almost the day after His Resurrection, people in the early church started emphasizing His Godliness and depreciating His humanity. This was the most convenient way to allow Him to be Savior without allowing Him to be Lord—to receive His grace without giving Him authority over everyday living.

People who know very little about theology still don't want Jesus to be human. They seem to intuit what that could mean—they would have to start becoming God, too!

I preached a sermon once that drew so much fire I thought I was done for. "Why is it," I asked, "that we use only a fraction of our mental capacity throughout our lives?" The average human uses about 5 percent of his or her potential. Geniuses use about 10 percent.

"What would happen if we had access to and used all of the reservoir? It's only speculation, but think about it. We know that the mind can affect the body where illness is concerned. With 'full access,' is it conceivable that we could detect and reverse disease?

"Matter is energy," I continued. "Objects are different composites of energy, which can be broken down. If we had 'full access,' could we use our energy to transport and teleport?"

Mouths hung open, but I pressed on. "What if the title 'Son of Man' meant a man with 'full access'? What if the result was the power to heal and vanish and reappear and walk through closed doors? And what if the Fall means the loss of 'full access'? And salvation the restoration of it?"

That's where I stopped. I have never heard such silence from a thousand people. "The reason you don't like this," I said, "is because you think it cheapens the image of our Lord."

"Amen!" said a dozen or more.

I continued, "You don't want Jesus' miracles to be explained scientifically. I'm making Jesus look like a Hollywood special effects man. Right?"

"Amen!" they said.

"And you think it's heresy to suggest that we might find

the capacity to do what He did?"

"Amen!"

"And you would rather I dropped this whole exotic fool-ishness and go back to conventional preaching?"

"Amen!"

And, Amen! We call this heresy because we are part of another heresy. We want Jesus to remain divine, and we ourselves to remain human.

The lady who called the next day said it all. "We're leaving the church. We discussed your sermon over lunch yesterday, and we decided that you see Jesus as a Superman! How dare you cheapen our beloved Savior!" Sad!

Hurrah for Scott Peck! He says we make Jesus 99.5 percent divine and 0.5 percent human. "Because the gulf is so great," says Peck, "American Christians are not seriously encouraged *to* bridge it. When Jesus said all those things about being the way... and that we were to be like him and might even do greater things than he did, he couldn't possibly have been serious, could he?... it is through the large scale ignoring of Jesus' real humanity that we are allowed to worship him in name without the obligation of following in his footsteps."[1] Jesus was the last Christian. The rest of us have a ways to go.

Chapter 4

BATTLES I NEED TO LOSE

A young man filled with the fear of missing his destiny, afraid he'll miss his train to greatness, goes to an island where hermits of God dwell. These are the ones who live in total spiritual concentration. They're called saints, gurus, mystics, monks.

He searches out the eldest and wisest. "Father," he asks, "do you still wrestle with the devil?"

"On no, my son," answers the wise man. "I am beyond that. Now I wrestle with God."

"You wrestle with God! But do you hope to win?"

"Oh no, I hope to lose."

There are battles I need to lose. I hate to admit it after having grown up in my Vince Lombardi world of victory worship. I could make you a long list, but really there are only two battles I need to lose—and both are with God. The rest are merely skirmishes in these two supreme conflicts.

One is the battle to cut God down to my size. I want a manageable God. One who fits my prescriptions for decency. One who reflects my political ideology. One who will stay in church where He belongs. One who will bless what I bless and curse what I curse.

For a long time I was a conservative evangelistic preacher, a hawker of packaged hot-gospel salvation. Like the rock 'n' rollers, nothing was worth hearing unless it was turned up loud. The first three rows needed a saliva shield when I got going.

I liked this kind of religion because it so easily confined God. The Bible—as I interpreted it—became my paper pope. In my world, the Bible and God were synonymous. The Bible was God! I was a preacher of the Bible. So I was God speaking!

What a deal! God was contained in my system. I could pull Him like a pistol and shoot whomever I chose.

Then I became a Christian intellectual. (It's a dangerous thing for a hot-gospel hawker to learn to read.) But no matter. I simply switched containers for God. Instead of locking Him up in my biblical interpretation, I confined Him to my rational understanding. God couldn't do anything contrary to Aristotle's logic. And I understood logic. My doctorate was in philosophy, after all. God was logic. I *was* a logician. Again, I was God speaking!

What a deal! I could still pull Him like a pistol and shoot the bad guys, who were mostly the hot-gospel hawkers shooting back at me.

Religious conservatives and liberals are really brothers under the skin. They both have manageable gods. That's why they fire at each other so often.

"Pigeon religion" is what I'm talking about. We whittle God down to our size so that we can pigeonhole Him neatly within the scheme we have devised for our lives.

It's not peculiar to me and my tradition, though. It's common to the whole human race. We do remake God in our own image. He's white or black, capitalist or socialist, remote or present, loves who I love—ad nauseam.

Idolatry is not just substituting one god for another. It is confining God to one place and time and culture and ide-

ology and structure. It is cutting God down to our size. In
the Bible, God is so picky about being idolized because He
refuses to be localized. Adam caves in when he is told that
if he eats the fruit, he and God will become the same size.
So do I!

The second battle is the flip side of the first. *It's the battle
to keep God from raising me up to His size.* I prefer to be
Superman—the most powerful of my species. I don't want
to be God-man. In fact, my religious tradition has conditioned me to cringe in fear at the mere suggestion that God
intends for me ultimately to become as He is.

But that's the message of Christ! He is the same as God.
To as many as received Him gave He the power to become
sons of God. It's in the Book!

But, as I said, I prefer to be Superman, not God-man. I
like power over, not power with. I really don't want to love
as God loves. I prefer to love conditionally. I prefer
revenge to forgiveness. I prefer to do in my enemies by giving them a dose of their own medicine. I prefer a limit to
my patience. Second chances are okay, but let's not get carried away with four or a hundred!

When I pray, "God help me to be a better person," I
don't mean, "Make me more like You." I really mean, "Let
good fortune come my way." Or, "Let others perceive me
as being a better person than they thought I was, because
being a better person gives me better standing among them."

Adam had the opportunity to grow, to become more
than he was, to evolve into oneness with God. But he chose
the Garden instead. He didn't want to be raised up a notch.
He liked running the Garden better than walking with
God in the Garden. So do I.

So, the two battles I need to lose are the battle to cut

God down to my size and the battle to keep Him from raising me up to His.

I haven't used the word "sin" here. It's not important to say the word. It's important to know what the word means.

Chapter 5

IF I WERE THE DEVIL

Pretend I'm the devil. What do I really like?

First, I like people to accept the portrait of me painted by Dante in the Middle Ages and refined by Hollywood. I like horns, cloven hooves, awesome rushes of wind—all the special-effects stuff. I like people to go into a cold sweat when they think of me. The more terror the better—vomit, scabs, 360-degree head-turns.

You see, that diverts people's attention. It allows me to move about in their lives undetected. If I can only get them to think I'm the prince of the ugly, they won't recognize me in the midst of the beautiful.

Most people still haven't caught on. They don't know that I always appear in the form of the pleasant and wonderful. C. S. Lewis, my great enemy, really nailed me when he said my first rule is to allure and entice.

I appear often at church. I'm the stained glass whose beauty diverts your attention just as you're about to hear a truth from God. I'm the pride your pastor feels when he or she wins a convert. I'm the satisfaction you feel when you gave 10 percent on Stewardship Sunday.

I really like people to be aware of how good they are. If I can just get you to focus on your goodness, I can destroy your humility. Humility is when you're good and don't notice it. It's goodness unaware of itself. I like you to *know* you're good. Then you become proud.

So please, keep thinking up good things to do and remind your self regularly that you did them. Get yourself some of those award plaques they give out at the service clubs. Hang them on the walls to remind yourself of the good things you've done. I just can't stand for you to be *unconsciously* good. Routine, unconscious service just scares the hell outta me!

Here's something else I like: people who think it takes magic to get rid of me. Incantations, professional exorcists, mumbo jumbo...I love it! People think they can take that stuff like medicine. A good dose of antibiotic and Satan's knocked out.

This is another diversion. It prevents people from dealing with me in the little matters of the everyday world. It makes me larger than life, a big problem instead of the sum total of all the little ones.

I really live in the millions of nuisances that plague people. If I can get you to restrict the battle to the big issues, I'm really cookin'!

I can't stand it when you fight me every day in the little moral arenas with prayer and confession and Scripture. It kills me when you're content to win an inch at a time instead of going for all or nothing. And when you really understand forgiveness, I hate it. Magicians, I love; consistency gets me.

I like to be blamed for all of your mistakes. It's a good way to program you for defeat. It gives me more credit than I deserve, and exonerates you from wrongdoing.

Flip Wilson is not my friend, because he makes a joke out of people who say, "The devil made me do it!" (I don't like laughter. It's the *real* anti-Satan vaccine.) I like people to take this seriously. The more problems you can blame on me, the more you will think that their remedy lies entirely outside your own will and effort.

This brings up God. I actually like people to "believe in God." That is, I like people to believe in the "Great Philanthropist Out There" the Force who started everything ticking and then removed Himself until the grand finale.

Do you begin to catch on? If you keep God "out there," beyond your reach, then you will think you have to fight me all by your self. Your wits against mine—that's the ticket!

The only time God ever gets in my way is when He gets involved personally in people's lives. But a removed and remote God is one of my best allies. People pay Him homage for a few hours once a week, or they mumble to Him at mealtime and when they're falling off to sleep. Otherwise, it's just me against them six-and-a-half days a week.

I like charismatic clergymen when they become vicarious heroes—when they live religious lives on behalf of their admirers. They don't have to be real. They only have to project a religious image. They're effective instruments in keeping people insulated from real religion.

Contrary to popular opinion, I have mixed feelings about guilt. I like one kind, but I hate the other. I like the kind that is placed on you by the people who are trying to change you into what they want to be, or think they are. I'm speaking of insecure parents, hot-gospel preachers, zealous social reformers, and the psychiatrists who make you feel guilty for feeling guilty and unhappy for being unhappy.

This kind of guilt imposed from the outside by people who want to make you "lovable" is the most wonderful assassin I know. It paralyzes its victims and kills them slowly.

They can't love themselves, so they can't love others. They can't ever do enough to gain the approval of those who impose upon them, because the imposers are guilty, too! They are only spreading around their misery.

And it is absolutely splendid when people think God is the Grand Imposer! When people begin to think they must improve themselves in order to earn God's approval, They are *mine!*

I like you to think you can earn God's love through exemplary performance. It's a nonstop guilt factory.

I hate the other kind of guilt. When you catch a vision of what you can be, and you compare it to what you are, I get nervous. When the self judges the self from the inside, the guilt that arises is good for you and bad for me.

It's good for you because it points you forward. It introduces you to your potential. You learn that God already loves you and is using this inward guilt as a tool to help you grow into His image.

Another thing: This inward guilt that you call "good" makes you immune to the guilt imposed upon you from the outside. That's bad for me. *Once you start letting God tell you who you are, I'm a goner.*

Which brings up the thing I like most of all, my highest ambition: I want people to let something created tell them who they are—friends, enemies, accomplishments, possessions, wives, kids.

Let me show you what I mean. I love it when a guy buys a Mercedes, not because it's a good car, but to show himself and others that he's reached the "Mercedes Club." The car tells him who he is. I love it when a mom lets her daughter's election as drill-team captain tell her that she's a great mom.

I love it when a young man lets only his ability to run with a football tell him he's "great." I love it when a social reformer allows his enemies to dictate his position on most issues. I love it when Christians build great institutions and then exhaust themselves worshipping their hallowed boxes. I love it when ministers allow their "ministerial image" to temper what they have to say.

You humans love to project images of who you think you are, and then you worship the images. These are the myths of superiority about your nation, race, economics, politics, and creed. If I can get you to worship these, I'm in the driver's seat.

But woe unto me if you start submitting all of these created myths to the Creator. *For Satan's sake, let anything but God tell you who you are!*

Chapter 6

LET'S HEAR IT FOR THE
"F"UNDAMENTALISTS

In the 1920s, most Americans were acquainted with the word *Fundamentalist*. It meant two different things depending on whether or not you were one.

If you were one, it meant militant devotion to the "Old-time Religion"—revivalism, temperance unions, and purging "modernists" (now called liberals) from the ranks of the faithful.

If you weren't one, it meant a certain "meanness" in the name of God—anti-intellectualism, and guilt-centered rigidity a la Sinclair Lewis's *Elmer Gantry*.

The Fundamentalists prevailed for a season—most notably in the form of Prohibition, and William Jennings Bryan's fight against Darwinism at the Scopes trial.

But Fundamentalism eventually failed for the same reason it always does. It tried to freeze time and God in its time. The result was an opposite reaction call the Roaring Twenties.

In the 1980s, the Fundamentalists have been at it again. They're riding the tide of a worldwide turn to the right (even claiming credit for it). They rule the religious airwaves and have made inroads into the political system.

They have ruled my denomination (the largest Protestant group in America) for ten years now. Their appeal is to those who yearn for something simple and solid in a sea of change.

But that's precisely where Fundamentalism always gets itself into trouble. It tries to make everything simple and solid. It tries to preserve the bath water as well as the baby.

So Fundamentalism will crumble again. But we don't have to react by moving to the opposite extreme. There is an alternative.

I'm a fundamentalist with a small "f." A Christian without fundamental, non-negotiable convictions is about as "useful as a bucket of warm spit" (as John Nance Garner described his vice-presidency). Along with Jeremiah, I believe we must "seek the old paths where the ground is solid and there find rest for our souls" (Jer. 6:16). There are parts of the so-called Old-Time Religion which are really the All-Time Religion.

I was once a card-carrying Fundamentalist—with the big "F"—I even scolded the wife of my first deacon chairman for wearing Bermuda shorts at the supermarket. My Fundamentalism had some interesting effects on my life, as the following stories show.

Lois and I were married six years before we were able to go on our honeymoon. One starry night as we strolled Waikiki, we came upon a luau with all of the romantic trimmings—an orchestra played, and there was a small portable dance floor occupied by only two couples.

Lois and I had loved to dance before I "surrendered to preach." When she suggested that we go for a spin, I looked at her as if she were Eve offering me an apple. We left promptly and attended a church service at Pearl Harbor.

I once declined an invitation to spend an afternoon with Paul Tillich, because a popular preacher with a D.D. said Tillich was a "dangerous theologian."

Then there was my Aunt Mary. She had eight kids, mostly by my uncle's previous marriages. She was a closet alcoholic. When she was hospitalized and dying, I asked her why she never came to me for help. "Oh, but I did!" she said. "I came one Sunday to hear you preach. I had decided to make a new beginning. Your sermon was entitled, 'The Case Against John Barleycorn.' You said a drunk couldn't get into the Kingdom of Heaven."

The Old-Time Religion wasn't what it was cracked up to be. Sometimes it was so silly that it scolded a man for dancing with his wife or a woman for wearing shorts. Sometimes it was so stupid that it kept young men from hearing great pioneers of the faith. And sometimes it was downright cruel. I could never go back to such tyranny. Nevertheless, every now and then, people like me need to remind themselves of the small "f's"—those basics that made the Old-Time Religion an All-Time Religion. Back in the 1920s Harry Emerson Fosdick often called himself back to the basics by preaching "A Fundamentalist Sermon by a Modernist Preacher."[2] I often use his theme to call myself back to the basics.

Martin Luther

When I think of great heroes of the faith like Martin Luther, I cannot believe many of the things he believed. He believed the earth was flat. He thought demons caused thunderstorms, because his childhood friend was killed by lightning. Once he threw his ink pot at the devil when he was unable to write his sermon properly. (That one I understand!)

Luther's defiance of Rome and proclamations of liberty

caught on with the German peasants. They thought they were people, too. But when they revolted, Luther sided with the nobles and thousands of serfs died. The German tradition of obeying orders without question was born, and we know where that led.

I reject these notions. But Luther had something I cannot reject. Fosdick called it an "unconsenting conscience." Luther had a loyalty to a living Christ that transcended his loyalty to anything else. When he discovered the New Testament and read it in Greek, he learned that people are made right with God by trust alone—no works, no rituals, no inherent goodness—just simple acceptance of God's acceptance.

Luther defied the Pope, the princes of the church, and even the Emperor of the Holy Roman Empire. I cannot go back to his outmoded doctrines, but God help me if I don't retain the center of his vision. It was the central vision of Jesus. He loved the Father more than he loved anything else.

Augustine

And what about Augustine, the great intellect of the church in the fifth century? Some of his beliefs seem quite ridiculous today. He was among the first to give in to the Greek notion that the affairs of the secular world must be separated from the affairs of the sacred. There was a "City of Earth" and a "City of God."

Again, thinking like Plato, he reasoned himself into the doctrine of predestination—every person's eternal destiny has already been decided.

It was Augustine who first equated the enjoyment of sexual union with sin (He gave us the notion that before the Fall, sex wasn't fun!). Although some people have never gotten over such nonsense, who but the intellectually suicidal could believe these things?

Yet Augustine had one old path we must find again and again: his radical conversion. After a decadent youth and forays into several religious philosophies, he had an experience with God in Jesus Christ that changed his life.

This experience became his central driving force. He could never discard it. Each of us has to know God firsthand if our religion is to retain its power.

That's All-Time Religion.

John Calvin

Then there was John Calvin, the intellectual and moral father of American Protestantism. In spite of his brilliance, however, some of his conclusions were carried to the absurd.

Calvinism carried predestination so far that it had babies crawling around on the floors of hell! Calvin rebelled against the Roman church's tyranny and turned around and formed one of his own.

He tried to enforce "prohibition" in the taverns of Geneva and was run out of town. After he accepted a plea to return, he led in the burning of a "heretic" named Servetus. It seems that Servetus didn't have his Christology down quite right.

I cannot associate with these excesses nor with their carryover into modern Fundamentalist witch-hunts. But Calvin had his solid ground, too. He had no illusions about humankind's ability to save itself. He knew there was something radically wrong with human nature—something that education, improved social conditions, political liberty, and economic prosperity could not cure.

Calvin knew that human nature needed redeeming by Divine nature. He knew that we cannot go spiritually and morally forward as a race unless we "leave the driving to God."

An unconsenting conscience; a commitment to first-hand religion; a realistic vision of the human condition and its cure—these are the *fundamentals* that are indispensable to any brand of powerful Christian faith. They are what make me a "f"undamentalist.

Chapter 7

WHAT'S THE BIBLE?

Why is the Bible the least-read bestseller in the world? Why do Christians fight over it? Why do all denominations, sects, and cell groups claim it as their authority for belief and practice? And then why do people end up believing and practicing so differently? Why do so many people find the Bible difficult to "get into" and "stay with"?

Well, there are a lot of reasons, but I want to focus on the main one. When most of us start trying to understand the Bible, we don't start with the right question: *What is the Bible?* We assume everybody knows what the Bible is, but they don't—even those who've read it from cover to cover and quote it profusely.

When you ask them what the Bible is, you get all kinds of answers. The most popular is, "It's God's Word." There are others: "It's a guide for living." "It's the Book about God." An eight-year-old said, "It's the book the preacher shouts from."

How would you answer the question? Your answer says a lot about how you approach the world with your religion.

For me, the Bible is the record of what God has done and is doing in history to reconcile all humankind to Himself. Each of the sixty-six books tells us something about this drama.

The first eleven chapters of Genesis tell why everything got started and what went wrong. Then the long process of

God's efforts to restore and right the ship of creation begins to unfold.

God decided to reach people with people. Actually, He started with one person—Abraham. Then He used a whole nation—Israel. The Old Testament is the record of God's attempt to use Israel as His agent of reconciliation. There we see God making a deal with His people. But then they break their part of the bargain. With that, He backs up and tries again. He tries through tribal patriarchs, deliverers, kings, prophets, priests, and so on.

The different types of literature in the Old Testament either chronicle or reflect on this redemptive effort. God's people experience deliverance. They are given laws to manage their society. They develop worship forms and rituals to remind them of God's redemptive actions in their past. Their poets and seers reflect on their experiences with God. And their prophets call them back to their roots.

When all of God's efforts to redeem people are thwarted, He makes His final move. He enters the human situation in the flesh. He takes the guilt and brokenness on Himself. He risks His own life as a human and the human wins! He goes all the way to death without giving in to the dark forces.

Christ dies in our place and God raises Him up. That's the drama of the four Gospels. The remainder of the New Testament is an account of what happened between God and the early church, the early believers' interpretation of it, and a grand vision of the end of things.

The Bible is one piece. It's the record of God's redemption of the human race. It contains moral lessons and laws. It speaks to every area of human life. It has poetry, allegory, and legends. But, as a piece, it is the record of the redemptive acts of God in history.

Now the questions flow hot and heavy. Is the Bible sacred? Is it purely a human document or is it imbued with divine spirit? Is it inspired? Does it have any errors in it? Are the creation accounts literal or symbolic?

Now, this isn't a book on the science of biblical interpretation, but here are some machine-gun answers. The Bible is inspired. God led the people who experienced His redemptive acts and the ones who later reflected on them to recognize them for what they were—Acts of God and not just happenstance. For example, many people witnessed the crucifixion of Jesus of Nazareth but only a handful recognized it as the culminating effort of God to redeem us. The rest of the people around the cross saw it simply as the execution of another troublemaker. The ones who saw God's involvement were "inspired."

The Bible is also inspired because God speaks to people through it now. People are still redeemed by reading the Scripture. But they are redeemed by God, not by the text.

The Bible is "sacred" in the sense that it serves as a transmission line from God to people and as a record of His former transmissions. But the Bible is not holy in and of itself. It is not God, but it is God's.

What about errors? It depends on what you mean by "errors." It is infallible concerning who God is; what He's up to; who we are; what we're meant for; the purpose and end of history—that is, in "matters of redemption."

But it is clearly not a science book. It doesn't tell us how God made the world, but why and where it's going. The two stories of creation in Genesis 1 and 2 are a good example. The first one focuses on the whole of creation, and the second on humankind as the crown of creation.

If you read Genesis in its original language, it is clear that the writer had a view of the universe that was commonly held centuries before Christ. The earth was flat with a dome over it—like a round cake-plate with a clear plastic cover. The dome held back the chaotic sea. Beneath the flat earth was the underworld.

What does this do to the truth of the creation accounts? I mean, we know the earth's not three-storied. If Genesis has to be scientifically correct, it's in trouble! But here's another way to look at it. First of all, the author of Genesis wasn't an eyewitness to creation. He didn't have a video camera.

Second, the creation accounts were probably compiled from ancient stories enduring the time of the Exodus from Egypt about 1500 B.C. Now hear this! The purpose of the writer was to nail down the truth that the God who had brought His people out of slavery and delivered them to the Promised Land was the same God who made the world out of nothing!

In other words, God created the world as the arena for fellowship with His own kind—that is, humans! How He created it isn't important; *that* He created it and *why* is the concern of Genesis.

Thus, scientifically speaking, the creation account is in error. But, speaking redemptively, it is true. I do not understand why scientists and religious practitioners continue their war.

I understand how it got started, though. The church had the universe figured out and the scientists started confusing them with the facts. Something had to give. Since the church had more muscle, it prevailed. The unfortunate result was that in order to use the scientific method of investigation, people had to revoke their faith.

The enmity still exists with amazing stupidity on both sides. Educated theologians and pulpiteers become scientists overnight and pronounce anathema on "satanic scientists." On the other hand, accomplished physicists become theologians overnight and summarily cancel all claims of religion as "superstitious nonsense."

I do not worship the Bible, so I am not afraid that a scientist will discover something the Bible can't account for. I worship the God whose actions and revelations were recorded by my spiritual ancestors. And I find that my own experiences with God are remarkably corroborated by theirs.

I believe that God is the source of all knowledge. What a generous gift to be able to unlock the secrets of the ages by way of any method—scientific or otherwise! And most certainly God has revealed marvels through the work of scientists.

The only quarrel I have is with the "irreverent ones" on both sides. The cocky preacher who struts to and fro as a know-it-all; and the smug intellectual who worships his method of discovering truth more than the truth itself.

I have said nothing about how to interpret the Bible. I haven't given formulas or mentioned original language, historical context, or the other principles of hermaneutics. These are important for the serious student of the Bible, but they are of little value if we don't know what the Bible is and what it's trying to do.

In the end, the Bible is valid only if God validates us. When that happens, it becomes food for the soul.

Chapter 8

BAD STUFF

"Bad stuff"—children with leukemia, adults who sexually molest children, earthquakes that exterminate, my own child sentenced to a life in silence when a measle virus attacked her in her mother's womb—this is the stuff I have to swallow in order to believe.

The traditional bad-stuff question is, "How can you believe in a God who is both all-powerful and all-loving and account for evil?" If He can stop it and doesn't, He's not all-loving. If He can't stop it, He's not all-powerful.

I've found that this question is valid only for the philosophers of evil and suffering. It's not the question most often asked by the sufferers themselves. After they go through the initial "Why?" stage, they want to know "How?" How can I live with this and through this? How can I find the energy to go on?

A lot of paper and ink have been wasted trying to explain God or explain Him away in the face of evil. It took a doctorate in philosophy for me to realize this. I wanted to know why my innocent child and I had been "chosen." I came away realizing that was the wrong question. We *had* been chosen. The questions were how to live with it and how to believe while I did.

Thirty years later, this is my first attempt to put my journey into words.

I won't try to share the pain of my suffering. Some of

you have suffered more. Besides, pain has no "degree" to it. Your suffering hurts you as much as mine hurts me, even if yours is, objectively speaking, "more severe."

The parent of a blind child asks me if I had rather my child have been blind than deaf. When I say I think blind would have been better, she tells me I'm nuts. I just don't understand. Then when I tell a friend whose child has died, "At least your grief-task is defined. Mine just keeps on going," he tells me I've lost my mind. A child alive is everything, he says.

The fact is that we all share the same gut-grinding, spirit-eating pain. So there's no need to compare whose is more or less painful.

I didn't go through the famous Kubler-Ross stages of grief—disbelief, anger, bargaining, acceptance, and response. Mostly, I've just cried a lot and gutted it out. But I still have a lot of questions I intend to ask God someday.

In all honesty, I don't think I have a formula for enduring suffering. The best I can offer is a few observations.

The only time I have been aware of God's real presence is when I look back, after time has frozen. He was there, but I didn't really know it. I felt no "overshadowing transcendence" or "special visitations," even though I sent out calls often enough.

The reason I know God was there is that I'm still here and I still believe. Several times I experienced what Geddes McGregor describes in *God Beyond Doubt*—when I accepted doubt as the absolute...when I got way out there on the skeptical fringe and believed nothing, I was strangely held together.

Don't get me wrong. There were no glorious revelations. I simply hung in there. Maybe it was the same experience

Sören Kierkegaard, the Danish Christian philosopher, described when he said he would like to let go of God but God would not let Himself be let go of.

I was given a lot of advice by well-meaning people. Only two really helped me. Dr. Empress Zedler, a salty child psychologist who had worked with the deaf into her late sixties, said, "You have to reserve a little place in your heart for the sad things." She understood.

Then there was Homer Hanna. When our daughter was twelve, we had to face the decision to send her away to school. We settled on Clarke School for the Deaf in Northampton, Massachusetts, twenty-five hundred miles from where we lived in West Texas.

We thought we had prepared ourselves well. But when it was time to leave her, I had to peel her fingers from around my neck. "Daddy. I love you. If you love me, no leave me here.

We flew home. The next day the doorbell rang. Homer said, "I just came over to cry with you." We did and he went on home. He understood, too.

Dr. Zedler and Homer Hanna were "God with me." I didn't know it at the time. I do now.

Another observation about the bad stuff: I found that it was so *bad* that I had to believe. You see, I started considering the alternatives. The atheists, Heideggar and Sartre and Camus, showed me what they were. If God is not, then all of life is absurd. The good stuff is even more cruel than the bad! If you love, you lose. Death comes along and nullifies all human happiness. Hell is other people.

What are we left with? Well, we can shake our fists at fate like Prometheus. We can accept the absurdity of it all. We can let our impending death purify our lives each day.

We can commit suicide.

Or we can keep believing that underneath it all, God is. We can live like he is there even when we can't feel his presence.

This has been my choice. On the face of things, it's a more realistic way to live than the nihilistic alternatives. But there is more. Now and then I *have* caught a glimpse. I feel like the lad flying his kite so high that he couldn't see it, he knew it was there because now and again he felt a tug.

Unfortunately for those of us who want God to submit Himself to our canons of reason, obedience always comes before understanding in His scheme of things. We have to believe, to hold on, to commit, before we can feel the occasional tug. It's tough, but that's the way it is.

The only rational explanation for bad stuff is a future solution. God has a lot of things to straighten out someday. There are injustices to redress. Maybe it's sentiment, but I believe God has "something special" in store for the "children of a lesser god."

In the end I must say that I have learned from the bad stuff. I know what it is to have only God and a handful of friends to depend on. I have learned that I am tough enough to endure sorrow. I have learned the inspiration of a child battling a handicap.

I have learned how to hurt and live over it. I have learned not only to accept risks but to welcome them. I have learned that one woman to love and bleed with for life ain't a bad way to live.

But I guess I haven't learned enough to be grateful for the bad stuff.

Chapter 9

WHY YOUR PRAYERS DON'T WORK

The slogans said, "Prayer changes things," "Be careful what you pray for, you might get it," "Ask and you shall receive." For years I prayed and prayed every day. And I preached sermons on prayer.

But, to be honest, I couldn't tell that it made much difference. I didn't get a hundredth of what I asked for. I felt better after praying, but I think it was because I had fulfilled an obligation. You always feel good after that.

I don't know how long it took me to realize that Jesus' disciples had the same problem. I had read Luke 11:1-13 many times before it dawned on me that they were asking Jesus, "Why don't our prayers work?"

He'd just returned from praying when one of them whimpered, "Why don't you teach us to pray like John taught his followers?" It was not really a question, it was a statement: "My prayers don't do for me what yours do for you! Tell me why."

Jesus' reply is strong. In short, He says, "Your prayers don't work because you don't know how to pray. Furthermore, you don't know who it is you're praying to, and you certainly don't know what to ask for."

Jesus handles the "how?" part by giving them a little sample prayer which has become famous and is known as "The Lord's Prayer." With all due respect, the focus should not be on the content, but on the method. "Pray like this,"

Jesus says. "Acknowledge God as a loving father whom you hope will become everybody's Father. Ask for what you *need*—food for a day, forgiveness, and the courage to dodge the traps."

Prayer is an exercise in acknowledging our dependence. We strengthen our cardiovascular systems by jogging, but we strengthen our spirits by depending. It's important to understand, though, that prayer is not begging, it's surrendering. Prayer changes the one who is praying, not the one who is being prayed to.

Matthew's account has Jesus adding that length, fervor, linguistic artistry, and audience have no effect on prayer. God doesn't need a hearing aid, either.

But the real focus should be on what Jesus says about the one to whom we pray. He says, we think we're praying to a God who is like a neighbor next door. It's late at night and a friend shows up at your house. Of course you want to feed him, but you're out of bread.

Your neighbor, who has bread, is already in bed and locked up for the night. You know he won't get up and give you bread just because he's your neighbor. But if you keep bothering him, he may get up and give in just to get rid of the nuisance.

In so many words Jesus says, "Your prayers don't work because you think God is like that cranky neighbor. He will give in to you if you just bother him enough."

"Not so!" says Jesus. "God is like you human fathers. You don't give your children snakes when they ask for fish, do you? And you don't give them scorpions when they ask for eggs? God knows what you need better than you know what your children need. So ask, seek, and knock. . . and then trust that He will give you what's best for you."

Point: Our prayers don't work because they are designed to change God instead of us.

Point: Our prayers don't work because we ask for what we think we need, instead of what God knows we need.

Point: Our prayers don't work because we don't know a "yes" when we hear one.

Chapter 10

Do It!

There is a scene in the movie *Gandhi* where a broken man enters weeping. He says to the Mahatma, "I have lost my soul. I am condemned to hell. The Muslims killed my family so I found a Muslim child and killed it."

Gandhi then tells him that he may yet be saved, if he will go out into the streets and find a little boy and raise him as his own son. Then, Gandhi adds, "But, you must raise him as a Muslim."

Gandhi was following the tradition of all of the religious masters. When people "found" themselves to be lost, they were given deeds to do rather than doctrines to believe.

This is certainly the biblical pattern. When John the Baptist announced that judgment was imminent, the people asked how they might be spared. He said in effect, "Do things that show you belong to God. Don't rest on your religious affiliation. If you have two shirts, give one to him who has none. If you have food, share it. . . . Tax collectors, don't collect more than is legal. . . . Soldiers, don't forcibly extract money, be content with your pay" (Luke 3:1-14).

Most of Jesus' direct instructions had to do with deeds, not doctrines. He even said that we would be judged by whether we did specific things like visiting prisoners and giving a cup of water. He announced that the tax collector Zacchaeus was "saved" because he pledged to give half his fortune to the poor and repay the 400 percent to people he had cheated.

What we believe will determine what we do. So doctrines are important. But what we do betrays what we believe. Therefore the word for Christians is, "Do it!"

Mend a Fence

For starters, *mend one old fence.* Get rid of an enemy by making up with him. Shakespeare had it right: To err is human. Anybody can hate, harbor resentment, lick old wounds. But to forgive is divine business. God has to be involved. Where there's making-up, there is God.

Forgiveness comes in different shapes and sizes. You can forgive the dead. A man told me one time that he'd finally forgiven his father who had been dead for seventeen years.

When I was eight years old, my hero was the Cisco Kid, Gilbert Rowland. One day I got to meet him backstage at the rodeo, and I was enraptured. He picked me up. I asked if I could hold his Mexican dagger. He gave it to me! It was my holy grail.

There was a bayou on one side of my house and a bully named Kenneth on the other. He was huge for his age and five years older than I. When I showed him Cisco's dagger, he scoffed and threw it in the bayou.

I hated him. I was helpless. During the following months, Kenneth's fighting roosters began to disappear. His dad's car threw a rod; sugar in the gas tank. But it wasn't enough.

Then Kenneth's father died. When the family came home from the funeral, Kenneth was last out of the car. As he walked to the house with his head down, I yelled, "Hey, fat boy, I'm glad your daddy died!" He ran into the house sobbing.

I knew something had happened. I felt a power unknown before. I sensed something dreadful yet intriguing. It was my fall from grace.

At twenty-eight, I tried to find Kenneth and make it right. I learned that he had died in Korea. My friend John Cobb told me that I could still mend my fence. I could receive my forgiveness from God. He was right.

Fortunately we can mend most of our fences with people who are present. Families can do it. Nations can do it.

Praise Someone You Know

For one week, praise two people you know each day and keep your mouth shut about the others. I don't know of a better way to do Christianity than to give affirmations, because we live in an *infirming* world, a world of put-downs, satire, repartee, one-upmanship.

America has turned into a junior high school slumber party, where the ritual is to dismember every classmate who isn't within earshot. Kenneth Erickson, in *The Power of Praise,* says the average child hears nine infirming comments to one affirming comment during the first seven years of his or her life!

Parents, peers, professors, coaches, and teachers still don't know that ridicule is not only ridiculous but evil.

If I praise two people a day and they follow suit in geometric progression, two million people would hear an encouraging word in three weeks! This is not a pep talk for salespeople. It's a powerful way to change the world.

Praise can be real. You don't have to fake it. It's not empty flattery. If you can't find something good to say about somebody, you're retarded.

Uh oh! Do you notice what I just did? In the name of affirmation, I criticized critics! Satan is alive and well.

Tithe

If I could recommend only one "do it" in modern America, I would choose one that sounds peculiar: *Give away the first ten cents of every dollar you receive to help someone.*

Tithing is the acid test of our commitment. I love the bumper sticker that says, "IF YOU LOVE JESUS, TITHE. ANYBODY CAN HONK!" In Christendom there's a lot more honking than tithing.

This is because God is Mammon. In New York, a visiting Indian guru saw the people rushing about Grand Central Station and asked his host, "What's wrong with these people? Is there a devil behind them?" "No," said the host. "There's a dollar in front of them."

Everyone laments the fact that America is in money-heat. University pundits are wondering what happened to ethics in business. (How soon they forget that twenty-odd years ago they ceased claiming responsibility for the student's ethical education!)

There is only one way to be a Christian with money. Give a proportion of it away.

I invited the most effective parent I knew to speak to my congregation about parenting. He began by reading them Malachi, the last book in the Old Testament. I was astonished. What did Malachi have to do with parenting?

He read Malachi 3:6-9, where God asks the people, "Do you think it's good to rob me? Well, that's what you're doing! 'How?' you ask. By withholding your tithes! You give me sick animals and bad corn. You find ways to cheat."

He closed the book and looked at the parents. "If I were serious about being a religious parent," he said, "I'd begin by tithing. Because you can't expect your kids to be honest if you cheat God on a regular basis."

I once went with the son of a deceased widow to gather personal effects and close her home. The boy began to thumb through his mother's checkbook. After every recorded deposit from Social Security, there was the first check made out to her church in the exact amount of 10 percent of the deposit. Then there were utility, food, and medicine payments. And finally there were gifts for the grandchildren and five TV evangelists.

The son said, "You know, the story of Mom's life is in her checkbook."

Check stubs speak louder than words!

All of the above "do its" won't help you find God. Nor will they make God love you more. Do them because God has already found you. Do them because you can help Him find others. Don't do it because you "ought" to. Do it because you want to.

Chapter 11

WHO THEY HAVE TO LISTEN TO

Since the televangelist scandals of the late 1980s, a general air of suspicion hangs over all aggressive evangelists. It's shakeout time. The white light of scrutiny has been cast on everyone who claims to have something of God to share. The world's ear is not lent as sympathetically as it was.

That's why we believers need to ask ourselves if we have anything to offer that the world cannot ignore. Are there people whom the world has to respect even if it rejects them?

Well, there used to be. You can read about them in the Book of Acts, chapters three and four. You can read about them here and there in history. In fact, some still survive today, although they're not peculiar to one church or religious group. Now and then, you'll find them in a group. Then they're really strong medicine. Yet they are mostly a remnant scattered.

But even so, this breed of people has a power about them that the world has to notice.

Changed People

The world has to notice *changed people,* people who radically alter the way they do life. You can call a changed life coincidental, but you can't call it unimpressive.

Simon Peter healed a cripple at the Temple Gate. The skeptics were confounded. They knew the guy. They had passed him daily for years. There he stood, whole.

But they were just as confounded by Simon Peter. They knew him, too. He was the one who had made all the noise about his allegiance to Christ and then fled. But this time he couldn't be bluffed. He was different.

You have to notice people like that. At seventeen I was sweet on a girl whose parents wouldn't let her go anywhere on Sunday except to church, so I started going to church. It was awful! Then one day it was announced that Wesley Hitt would teach a Sunday school class for high school boys beginning the next Sunday. I knew Wesley Hitt! Never had anyone been more appropriately named. He hit everyone he saw when he was drunk, which was every chance he got!

I went to see. He saw me come in. "Now, boys," he said, "before we start the Bible lesson I have to tell you that I know that some of you know how I used to be. I ain't goin' into no details, but I just want to say that I ain't like I used to be. I ain't nowheres near perfect. But I ain't nowhere's near like I was, neither. I have a new life. I hope you'll stick around long enough for me to prove it to you."

I held on to my unbelief for several years. But I couldn't ignore the life of Wesley Hitt, the changed one. He made a difference.

I think it was William James who went with his college roommate to hear a famous atheist debunk God. As they left, the roommate said, "Well, I guess that about does it for God." "No," said James, "He still hasn't explained the powerful faith of my elderly aunt in Massachusetts." One powerfully lived life cancels a multitude of rational arguments.

Brave People

They have to listen to *brave people*—those who risk, those who stand up and take it. Peter, James, and John—all former cowards—suddenly became un-cowed. When they were told to shut up, they said, "You can decide whether you think we should heed you or God. We've decided to keep on speaking."

This was no Sunday school debate. Their lives were on the line. But they kept on telling what they'd seen and heard (Acts 4:13-20).

You have to notice people you can't threaten.

Christians aren't persecuted anymore. In fact, church affiliation looks good on a resume. So what do "brave believers" look like today? They're people who are faithful—to their mate, to their friends, to their job.

A brave believer is Charles, who sits in our congregation every Sunday and sings and listens and even takes notes to keep from falling asleep when the sermon's bad. Charles is a professional man, educated and successful in business. But now he's lost his business and his health. He is a past–mid-life architect losing his sight and with a bad heart. Not exactly your star witness for a positive-thinking seminar. Right?

Wrong! You can't whip Charles. It's his faith. He knows God other than by hearsay. Guts! That's what Charles has. They have to listen to Charles.

People with Scars

They have to listen to *people with scars...* people who've been there. They had to listen to Peter because he was telling them what he'd "seen and heard." He wasn't trying to sell them a soft drink he himself hadn't drunk! He spoke from experience, not opinions gathered from someone else's reported experience.

On TV last Sunday I heard a "sermon" read from a manuscript by one of those stand-sideways-in-the-pulpit-and-look-bilious boys. I heard another shouted by one of those stand-on-the-pulpit-and-spray-spittle-on-the-first-row boys.

The bilious brother quoted (count 'em) seven philosophers, three theologians, and one cartoonist in twenty minutes. The crowd shots showed a congregation trying hard, with glazed-over eyes.

The spittle brother quoted the Bible (count 'em) eleven times and *Playboy* magazine once. But the crowd shots were identical—trying hard, with glazed-over eyes.

The medium was different—one studious and the other stupendous. But the message was the same. Both brothers were preaching someone else's opinions.

The world isn't waiting with bated breath to hear what Kierkegaard said about worship. And the world doesn't lie awake nights pondering what Moses did to the Jebusites. They don't have to listen to secondhand opinions. They do have to listen though to people who've been there and can show their scars! They want to know what God said to you, not to Moses and Kierkegaard.

Generous People

They have to listen to *generous people*. The members of the early church did something so radical they couldn't be ignored. They defied the god Mammon (the god of getting and keeping money). "No one in that crowd said that his belongings were his own. Instead they all shared every-thing" (Acts 4:32). They decided to have their money and not to be had by it.

People have to listen to people who put their money where their mouth is. Jesus said you can find a man's heart in his pocketbook (Matt. 6:21, "Your heart will be where your riches are").

Today we've gotten real cute with our "religious giving." Church boards are filled with people who cheat God on a regular basis because, "What a person gives is strictly between him and God."

Not so in the early church. Barnabas sold his farm and donated the proceeds. Gifts were a matter of record for someone besides the tax collector. Annanias and Sapphira tried to cheat and dropped dead!

They can call generous people deluded, but they can't turn a deaf ear. I'm thinking of Jeanie—single parent of three. She has no child support, holds down two jobs, and has one teenager in the hospital. There she is every Sunday, teaching a class or gathering clothes for the "underprivi-leged." The first check she writes on payday is to her church. She doesn't talk much. But when she does, people ignore E. F. Hutton.

Radiant People

They have to listen to *radiant people.* I don't mean the gushy sentimentalists (although they are preferable to the long-faces). I mean those who emit that "something" which you know is real.

It's the something referred to in Acts when the writer said that great grace was upon them all (Acts 4:33).

Mega-karis, mega-grace—people radiate that if they have it. It can't be ignored. D. M. Stanley, the agnostic reporter who went to find Dr. Livingstone in Africa, said, "If I had stayed with Livingstone much longer, I would have been compelled to become a Christian, although he never mentioned a word of his faith to me."

They have to listen to radiant people. Yet someone somewhere introduced the notion that religious presence must be repulsive instead of magnetic. You get the feeling that some of us were baptized with insect repellent.

I was once asked to be a speaker at a prestigious retreat center. I arrived "full of the spirit," only to learn that the other speaker—and also my roommate—was a Roman Catholic priest.

I had learned my anti-Catholicism well. I was convinced that the Roman Catholic church was the longest-standing monarchy in the world. It used superstition and fear to impose bondage on its victims. It had its own misery factory, banning birth control and thereby guaranteeing its own prolongation. From my point of view, a man had to commit intellectual suicide to be a Roman Catholic cleric. The last thing I wanted was to share room and podium with one of "them."

Then Father Keith Hosey ruined it all. He was a "radiator." He had that different glow. He had scars. He had guts. He was generous. I was silenced. Then I was drawn. All of my ill-conceived prejudices melted. He was my brother because we had the same Father, the same sin, and the same Savior.

I had to listen.

The same goes for my experience with Abraham Heschel, the great Jewish teacher. He also destroyed my prejudices in a matter of hours even though I was a young doctoral student with all of the answers! He knew the same God I thought I knew.

Again I had to listen.

Chapter 12

NOTCHES AND SCALPS

In 1976, when presidential candidate Jimmy Carter told reporters he was a "born-again Christian," most of them didn't know what the phrase meant. But according to the Gallup Poll, 65 percent of American Christians did.

I certainly did. I was birthed and suckled in Carter's religious tradition, where the central obsession is individual evangelism—confronting people with the decision to make a personal commitment to Jesus Christ. "Being born again," "gettin' saved," "accepting the Lord"—these are the Baptist buzzwords.

As I mentioned in chapter 1, I had a life-changing encounter with God when I was twenty. It was so stupendous that even today trying to put it into words is like trying to "scoop up the ocean in a teacup," to quote Joy Davidman.

So naturally I fitted right in with the Baptist tradition. Getting "as-many-as-I-could, as-fast-as-they-would" to have the same experience became my passion. My motives were as sincere as any hot-hearted young minister's could have been.

I soon realized that the top of the success ladder in my denomination was reserved for those who had "won the mostest the fastest." I began to measure my self-worth—and more important, my God-worth—by "how many, how fast."

The result was predictable. I sincerely and innocently became an accomplished manipulator. I began to count converts like the bounty hunter counts notches on his gun or the warrior counts scalps on his lodge-pole.

I became skilled in evangelistic methods. I'd stand 'em up with every head bowed and eye closed. Then I'd say, "If there's someone here tonight who's not 100 percent certain that he'd go to heaven if he died tonight, raise your hand. God bless you. I see that hand."

I arranged "altar calls" (that's the challenge to accept Christ and come forward at the end of the sermon) with studied aplomb. I even rehearsed voice inflection and tears. I used fear and guilt. I even learned how to "draw and net" in the six-to-eight-year-old Sunday school departments.

Now, years later, it is easy to poke fun at the people who still use these tactics. It helps assuage the guilt I feel for having used them myself. But I know where these "evangelists" are coming from. And besides, it was just this sort of high pressure manipulation that first started me to thinking about my relationship to God.

I can never go back to this kind of warped vessel, but the truth is, I was once a notch on a pastor's gun and a scalp on an evangelist's tentpole. God can use our methods in spite of us. And evangelism is part of the highest calling of the church. Jesus told us to "make disciples." Well, it's impossible to make 'em if they ain't been born to start with! Every person *does* have to be "born again" if he or she is to be of much use to God.

The question is, how—by what means? When is evangelism legitimate? All I have to offer is what works for me. I have seen many people enter the Christian way without the high-pressure manipulation I described above.

Some basic ingredients must be present in a church that reaches converts on a continuing basis and with integrity. First the church has to be concerned with making people whole rather than holy. The biblical words "salvation" and "saved" come from the root word meaning "healthy" or "whole." To be "saved" means to be made whole.

This means the church is not a shopping mall for religious consumers...a superstore with an inventory to supply every need. Nor is it a spiritual fitness center where saints come regularly to stay in shape while awaiting their portage to heaven.

The church is a rehab center for the broken, battered, beaten, and bored. Its business is healing.

And people *want* to be healed. Every human has a natural yearning for wholeness. But we keep this yearning at bay if we feel that we're going to be exploited or manipulated in some way.

The churches keep forgetting this very simple fact: *People want to be healed and they will submit themselves for healing, if they are accepted and loved without condition!*

So here's the first ingredient of honest outreach: The church must offer the people who come within its orbit a minimal guarantee—a limited warranty—that they will be accepted and forgiven, no matter what.

We must accept people as they are, where they are. The church must be an inclusive open-arms community, a family of sinners, a place where people don't have to pretend. Where there is safety, people let down their defenses. And, when defenses are removed, there is a natural tendency toward healing.

Then comes the second ingredient of evangelism: sharing only what has been experienced—one beggar telling another beggar where he has found bread. No canned spiel is required. No soul-winning schools. Simply each person telling his or her own unique story.

We see hundreds of people converted each year without evangelistic crusades and trained salespersons. Many ask to be baptized. Three-fourths of these are adults. I am convinced that the fertile ground for God to meet people person-to-person is provided by (1) removing all of the threatening symbols of traditional evangelism and providing a safe accepting community and (2) telling no more than one's own experience.

You don't have to make people feel guilty. They'll manage quite well on their own. You don't have to make people want to be whole. Simply remove the fear, tell your story, and let God have the notches and scalps.

Chapter 13

WHY I'D GO TO CHURCH
IF I WEREN'T A PREACHER

I'm not amazed that so many people don't go to church. I'm amazed that so many do!

Sunday after Sunday, there they are. They endure much—getting ready, fighting on the way, trying to keep all of the kids pacified, trying to stay with the preacher all the way through the sermon, having to wait behind the Presbyterians in the cafeteria line (they always start their services a quarter of an hour early).

Frankly, I have asked myself many times whether I'd go to church if I weren't a clergyman—that is, if I didn't have to. Would I get involved in the ministries I ask my people to support? Would I come every week to listen to me? Would I give my Saturdays to drive nails for a ghetto renovation project? Would I attend choir practice until 10:00 P.M. on Wednesdays?

In all honesty, I would! I would go to church for the same reason they come. There is really only one reason, although on a conscious level most churchgoers don't know what it is.

If you asked them why they go to church, they'd give you any number of answers: habit, to be close to God, to feel good, to recharge my batteries, to learn more about God, to be with my friends, to find spiritual strength.

These are excuses, not motives. I don't know why we

continue to overlook the truth about churchgoing. People go to church and will always go to church *because God has willed it! The church is not God, but it is God's.* There will always be some kind of gathered, institutionally shaped body of believers because that is God's plan.

In our desire to build ecclesiastical monuments to ourselves, we can think up a thousand excuses for church affiliation. But the truth is that the church's fate and future never depended on us.

Jesus made this clear in Matthew 16:18. The church's purpose is devil demolition, to "knock down the gates of hell." The church is God's wrecking crew wherever it gathers—in the dale, in the bush, in the cathedral, at Fourth and Main, or "wherever two or three..."

The church is people, not place. They are to knock down the gates with salt and light—to preserve their community from decay, (salt keeps things from rotting), and to expose all of the dark places where Satan hides.

Millions of churchgoers couldn't tell you what I've just said if you asked them. But most of them sense it somehow. They intuit that church is "more" than social and organizational and activistic and devotional. Even with all of its warts and pimples and outmoded drudgery, there is a power there that makes a difference.

I'd go to church if I weren't a clergyman. Not because the churches I see and serve excite me any more than they excite you. I'd go because that's what God's people do when they are salt and light.

Of course, there are many people who believe and pray to God and never "darken the door." What of them? They are salt and light, too. They can't stop as much rot and light as much darkness. That's a pity. So much power going to waste. It is stronger to come together.

Don't worry about the church. God will see to it that the church not only survives, but conquers. Worry about "which side of the gates" you're on.

Chapter 14

WHERE I'D GO TO CHURCH
IF I WEREN'T A PREACHER

As a minister, I haven't had the privilege of choosing which churches to join. I have had the privilege of leaving a few—by choice and otherwise. But if I were church-shopping, here's the church I'd join.

First, it would be *a church where people could sin "in front of each other."* The first requirement for membership would be to acknowledge sinfulness. That way, you could get all of the strutting pretense cleared up at the start. Every person could admit he or she was a hypocrite on at least one subject, and be done with having to hide from fellow hypocrites.

I'd like it if confession of specific sins were okay. Of course, you'd have to have some limits on that, or the place would be packed with folks who were just curious.

Alcoholics Anonymous is the model for the church I'm thinking of here. You can't come if you're not a drunk, and healing begins with acceptance and confession. Yet the purpose is not to come and brag about being a drunk, but to get well.

This brings up the second requirement on my church-shopping list. I'd join *a church where you either get well or get out.* To be "saved" means to be becoming whole. Some sick folks come to church and make everybody else sick. They even get to be on the Board because they groan and gripe. I'd want a church where people could get well instead of sick.

There are two fundamental parts of a healthy church's strategy: *grace* and *grit*. Some people call them *affirmation* and *expectation*. The strategy goes like this. Sinners are welcome. People are accepted right where they are, as they are. The only requirement is a willingness to "get well," to grow toward the image of Christ.

The critics who demean the church for being the "easiest club in the community to join" are actually telling it like it ought to be! The church should be the most open-armed organization in the world! If you're "sick" and you want to "get well," you're welcome! That's unconditional love. That's grace.

Then comes grit. God has not called us to be healed and then to sit. He has called us to be "healed healers." So the second part of the strategy is to *grow people, to demand that they be a responsible part of the family.* If they do not want to grow, we should not.continue to bless their fixations.

Jesus accepted everyone, but not everyone stayed. You either started to get well or you got out. Expectation wasn't separated from affirmation. There was no grace without grit.

That brings me to the third thing I'd look for in a church. *I'd join a church that isn't afraid to convert its own members.* Gordon MacDonald was playing my song when he said every church that has a vital spiritual passion will attract five kinds of people:

1. VRPs—Very resourceful people who inspire the dream
2. VIPs—Very involved people who share the dream
3. VTPs—Very teachable people who catch the dream
4. VDPs—Very draining people who sap the dream
5. VNPs—Very nice people who enjoy the dream[3]

The VNPs are the largest group. Like "smiling cereal," they just lie there and sop up the milk! They will take all you can give them. All they give in return is a big ego to the preacher, because they fill up the sanctuary on Sunday.

But the "20-80 rule" is reality: 20 percent of the congregation gives 80 percent of the money and does 80 percent of the work.

The church must acknowledge this reality without blessing it. The trick is not to curse the VNPs, but to nudge them constantly. There are really two churches in every church—the VRPs, VIPs, VTPs, and the rest. I'd join a church that recognized that a major part of its mission was to convert its own congregation!

I'd join a church where the preacher had what our Jewish friends call "chutzpah"—an earthy word for courage. Almost all preachers look like they do. But that's deceiving. Often the ones who shout and scream the most are the biggest cowards.

For example, in my denomination I drop in on a preacher's conference about every five years to see if they're still saying the same thing. Sure enough, they are! Fearlessly they are upholding the Bible, motherhood, and soul-winning—to their clones! Talk about safe subjects!

Preachers with chutzpah don't preach to the choir. They're not afraid of losing their jobs. They have nothing to lose. They don't have to control all of the committees, and they don't speak the "language of Zion" in the "tones of Cathedra." Instead they say, "I don't know," and, "I've changed my mind about that."

I'd join a church where they have fun. The number one requirement for worship would be to celebrate with a laughing God. I'd like to feel good about me and the world when I worshipped. I'd like not only to know I'm okay and you're okay, but that *it's* okay—that in spite of all of the mess, God is alive and well and in charge of reality. I am weary of preachers preaching to themselves, and choirs singing to themselves, and "liturgical-dirgical."

I'd join a church where God has no grandchildren. He doesn't, you know. Every one of us must be conceived by His Spirit. We must know Him for ourselves. There is no faith by proxy. "God is alive," we say. Why not meet Him, then?

Finally, I'd join a church that judged itself by the difference it makes in its world. We seldom get around to this standard of measurement. To do so would expose our pitiful mediocrity. We point to buildings, budgets, and baptisms to measure our effectiveness. But the test of our mettle is the spiritual and moral difference we make in our little corner of the world.

Is the church making any difference in the social fabric of its society? In most communities, most churches simply coexist with the government, the schools, and the business establishment. Even if the movers and shakers are also church members, they often live like spiritual schizoids. Religion and commerce do not mix.

The church's mission is not to reserve a haven for the righteous, a "safe house" where the saints wait for the train to heaven. Its mission is to penetrate and swell up the dough.

One more thing. No doubt I'd have a hard time finding a church if I waited for one that met all of these requirements. As a matter of fact, I wouldn't wait. I'd either join one that was willing to reach for these goals or gather up a small group and start one.

Chapter 15

THE PRIESTLY CLASS

As a kid the only minister I ever knew very well was Preacher Cole. I don't know if he had any other name. That was what everybody old and young called him. Not "Preacher" or "Brother Cole" or "Rev. Cole," but both names as one—"Preacher Cole."

He took in my father in the 1920s, when Dad was a twelve-year-old runaway in the Trinity Riverbottoms of East Texas. Preacher Cole wore overalls, chewed tobacco, cussed a blue streak, and knocked down three quail on every covey-rise. He was famous for whippin' rowdy drunks and church troublemakers with his fists. He served the same rural church for thirty years and was adored by the oddest assortment of renegade parishioners.

He had no minister friends. When I asked him why, he said, "The priestly class is the worst thing that ever happened to the Cause. They're like cockroaches. It ain't what they pick up and carry off, it's what they fall into and mess up." (Years later, coach Darrell Royal of the University of Texas made this old saying famous.)

I asked him why he was one of them, then. He said, "'Cause God won't let me do nothin' else—dammit!"

Now I'm one of them too—and for the same reason. And I don't know a minister who doesn't feel that he has a mandate from God. But I've never forgotten Preacher Cole's analogy. The fouling of the nest by the priestly class is well documented.

Remember Aaron? His brother Moses left him to tend the people while he went to the mountain for "further instructions" from God. When Moses stayed too long, Aaron decided that the believers "needed some new symbols to remind them of God." (Does that sound familiar?) So he made the golden calf.

And there's Eli. He and his sons became the elite God-practitioners. It took a child named Samuel to correct them, but not until they'd fouled the nest, too.

The Old Testament prophets had a running battle with the professional clergymen who kept "falling into and messing up."

Jesus was done in by the clergy. The priestly princes had fiefdoms to defend. They couldn't be deterred by new facts. Christ wasn't in the catechism, so he had to go.

Abraham Maslow has tracked the world's great religions from a psychological perspective. He says they all commence with a charismatic figure who has had a "peak experience" an experience with "transcendence." I think Maslow means a vision of universal proportions—a dream of uniting humankind, a unique set of insights that suddenly brings all of the fold together in a new way. We'd call it an encounter with God.

No matter. Here's the important point: the "peaker" shares his experience with his or her immediate contemporaries, and this vision is contagious. The peaker's cohorts have the peak experience too! The contagion grows like wildfire as new peakers catch the vision.

But after a while the non-peakers move in. These are the professionals who are compelled to consolidate the gains that have been made by the early peakers. They collect all of the testimonies of the peakers and see that they're written down.

Soon rules for "peaking" are established. Tests are devised for measuring whether communicants have truly had peak experiences. Rituals for rehearsing, celebrating, and creating peak experiences are born. Then this whole body of testimony, rules, and rituals is interpreted into a logical whole, usually called a "creed."

And the creed has to be guarded, preserved, and prolonged. Keepers have to be ordained. They are called the clergy, the priestly class.

They—we—are the ones who fall into God's doings and mess them up. Major battles are being waged in almost every branch of Christendom. Methodists, Baptists, Lutherans, and Catholics are going at it. The same battles are raging in Islam, Judaism, and Hindustani.

I don't know of a case, however, where the fight isn't really among the priestly princes. In my own denomination, the laity is trying to find and be found by the God of nine-to-five, while the ministers are fighting over strained gnats.

Is the answer fumigation? What would happen if the clergy were demoted or even "exterminated"? *We would immediately commence to rebuild what we just got rid of!*

The folks who knew God firsthand (the peakers) would become leaders who would attract disciples, who would attract organizers, who would standardize "peaking" all over again! A new priestly class would emerge!

Great religious movements have never lasted very long without the involvement of the laity. It's always easy to hire someone to minister. And it's equally easy for the hired man to become a courtesan of the laity's pleasures. In order to keep power, the clergyman has to pander. If prostitution is the oldest profession and politics the second oldest, the ministry can't be far behind!

Ministers are going to have to trade success for service.

Upward mobility is alive and well in the ministry. Preachers don't use drugs and drink, they "snort" success...the big church...the big crowd...leading the march...being published...invocations at prestigious meetings...and television!

I've just read John Keller's book, *Let Go, Let God*.[4] I was humming along through his explanation of how the Alcoholics Anonymous program was really the gospel in drag, when he stabbed me with the term "success addiction"—people get high on success like they get high on booze. It's rewarding. It gives you power. But it's like crack cocaine. Every time you come down the down is lower. And every time you go up, the high is lower.

Then Keller twists the knife when he comes along with the idea that if you're a minister you attribute your success to God and have the best of excuses to neglect your family and your people. ("Sorry, I can't do your husband's funeral. I'm speaking at the national convention of funeral directors in Milwaukee. But you'll be very much in my prayers.")

Then he killed me dead when he said, if a preacher who is hooked on success has a heart attack (and I did!) and is told by his doctor to slow down, he simply has no way even to comprehend what that means. He usually gets out of bed and proceeds to kill himself.

We clergy will continue to foul the Kingdom until we become laity again. The word "laity" in the Bible simply means "people of God." There's a place for the clergy, but it's not as an elite class.

Here's the best description of our place that I've heard. An elderly pastor was asked to describe his sixty years in the ministry. He said that he saw his ministry in three phases.

In the first phase, he saw his people as if they were in this river drowning. His job was to stand on the bank and tell them how to get out of the river.

In the second phase, he saw himself as edging down the bank to the water's edge, leaning over and pulling them out of the river.

Finally, he got in the river with them. As they were swept toward their destiny in God, they held onto each other and paddled like crazy.

Those three kinds of preachers can be found holding forth on any Sunday. There are those who stand high and dry on the high bluff of righteousness, shouting "divine" warnings and instructions on how to climb out.

There are those who have turned their task into "reaching down" to the oppressed and helping them to their social rights.

And there are those who have jumped in with the rest of the sinners. They are clinging, clutching, and treading water like crazy.

If you don't want to "fall in and mess up," you have to "jump in and hold on."

Chapter 16

ARE WE STILL COUNTIN'
NUMBER SEVEN?

Then there's the story about the end of the world. Folks are lined up for miles at the Pearly Gates waiting to see if they qualify for admittance. The line moves up and stops, moves and stops. All of a sudden the people at the back of the line hear this commotion up at the gate. There's whooping and shouting and trumpets. The word filters back, "They're not countin' adultery!"

When it comes to the Ten Commandments, I'm afraid we haven't been countin' number seven for a long time. Oh, Ingrid Bergman's career was hurt by it years ago, but then Liz Taylor and Richard Burton ushered in the Hollywood era of "making it" by breaking it. Adultery actually enhanced one's career. Even civil rights leaders and presidents weren't called to task for it.

Then there was the fuss made over Hart, Bakker, and Swaggart. But that didn't mean we started counting the Seventh Commandment again. The fact is, there's "a whole lotta fornication goin' on!" (When they asked a televangelist the difference between fornication and adultery, he said he'd tried 'em both and couldn't tell any difference.)

But, all joking aside, our society is sexually confused. The Seventh Commandment is taken about as seriously as the Tenth (Thou shalt not covet).

I'd like to address the causes, though, not the symptoms.

Why do so many people find it unnecessary or impossible to practice sexual restraint and faithfulness in relationships?

There are two big reasons. A lot of little ones stack on top of the two. One is that millions of otherwise bright and useful folks haven't the slightest idea about the real secret of lasting relationships. They don't know what loving is.

I'm not going to argue this point. It's as obvious as saying everybody breathes air. Nor am I going to lay out a formula on how to build, fix, repair, and sustain relationships. We have enough marriage manuals.

There isn't really any great mystery to a lasting relationship. It takes only two things: the decision that it will continue, and the continuing decision that it will continue. In other words, *commitment* and *more commitment.*

People become adulterous when they are no longer committed. When they lose their nerve to hang on for dear life, to be faithful when it's no longer fun, to keep the old jalopy when the fenders get bent and the upholstery frazzled. In a society where convenience, shallow relationships, and a passion for the "new" are the order of the day, why should we be surprised to see the same trend show up in our "sleeping habits"?

The reason marriages "used to last" is that people were committed. They weren't necessarily more moral than we are; they just had fewer options. Marriage was a life sentence. When trouble arose, your options were to solve it or bear it. When Charlie got Janice pregnant, it was "until death do us part"—*us,* not the *fetus!*

Now we're free. Free not to be committed. Free to steal our neighbor's spouse.

The second big reason we're not countin' seven anymore is because of *de-cadence.* Without the hyphen, the word is a preacher's word. It reeks of scorn and judgment—as in, "a decadent society bound for the fires of hell."

But de-cadence really means the loss of cadence, of a basic rhythm in the march of life. It means to be out of step, unsynchronized, offbeat. You can't hear the drum, much less march to it.

When people are without a cadence, they get bored. They don't have anything much to do. And sometimes when people don't have anything to do, they go to bed with somebody. A man without a purpose—without a drum to march to—needs a sweet young thing to tell him he still has some fire in his britches.

The sweet young thing needs to prove her mettle in the ranks of the newly liberated. She doesn't *feel* liberated. Nine-to-five ain't what it's cracked up to be. She also needs "notches on her gun" to tell her she's somebody.

So we're not countin' number seven because we're not committed and because we're bored. We're de-cadent. We have no drum to march to.

We won't start countin' seven again until we learn to count to one ("Thou shalt have no other gods before me"). Adultery doesn't destroy society. It is the symptom of a society that is destroying itself. Adultery doesn't destroy a marriage. It is the symptom of a marriage that is already destroyed.

Adultery is not sin, it's *one* of the sins that derives from sin—the condition of being without a "One" before which there is no other.

To make seven count, you have to count to One.

Chapter 17

GREAT SEX FOR CHRISTIANS

Twenty years ago, I announced that I was going to preach a sermon entitled, "Great Sex for Christians." The place was awfully full and awfully quiet.

I began with the old joke: "Sex is great on days that start with 'T'—Today, Tomorrow, Tuesday, Thursday, Thaturday, and Thunday!"

There wasn't even a titter, let alone laughter. Just gasps. Those folks had never heard the words "great" and "sex" and "Christians" mentioned in the same sentence. Sexual enjoyment was the curse of the Fall, the aftertaste of Eve's forbidden fruit.

Today, when I announce the same topic, the place is just as full and just as quiet before I speak. They laugh at the joke now. They've been through the so-called "sexual revolution."

But the sad truth is that they are as unable to relate their sexuality to their spirituality as their predecessors were. They still labor under the illusion that they either have to love sex and hate God, or hate sex and love God.

How do I know? Because they are unable to sustain relationships. Because they're lonely. Because they've been "liberated" to solitude and the inability to be committed. Or because they are still uncomfortable to hear about sex from the pulpit. Or because their sexual relations are meaningless.

Great sex occurs when sexuality is blended with spirituality. One without the other leaves half a person. How are sex and religion related?

God Created It

In the Bible, the first word about human sexuality is that God created it. And the second word is that it was "good." In fact, it was more than good. In Genesis 1 and 2, everything created before sex is called "good" the land, the plants, even Adam, who is androgynous (male and female in one). But when God splits humanity into male and female—when He creates sexuality—He calls it "very good"!

So the first key to great sex is to realize that it is God's gift. I like to think that when Adam saw Eve for the first time, he said, "At last, dear hearts, at last!" And with that we learn why a man leaves his father and mother and joins with his wife, and the two become one flesh.

If sex is God-given, then *anything a couple enjoys sexually that is not damaging or forbidden in Scripture should be celebrated as a gift of God.*

Here's another one: *Any couple who settles for dull, mechanical sex is going against God's purpose for creation.* I'm amazed at the narrow definition we give to the word "infidelity." I have had couples come to me in hysterics because one of them has had an affair, but then I discover they're not disturbed in the least to tell me that they've had a monotonous sex life for years!

Infidelity means unfaithfulness. But unfaithfulness means more than extramarital sexual intercourse. The man or woman whose lovemaking is devoid of fantasy, imagination, and experimentation is being unfaithful to God's gracious gift.

Sex and the Image of God

The second key to great sex is to realize that our sexuality is a reflection of our kinship with God, not a reflection of our kinship with the lower animals. Actually, what differentiates us from the animals is our capacity for intimacy, for blended relationships with God *and* with each other. "Image of God" means capable of relationships with other people.

Sex is a means by which union with another person occurs. It's the bridge to at-one-ness. This means that about all we can learn from studying the sexual behavior of animals is more about the sexual behavior of animals!

It also means that sex is not a basic drive. It's only the symptom of our primary need—the need to fuse with someone outside ourselves, the need to cure what philosophers call "existential loneliness." Those are big words to describe the fact that we know we're separate and we yearn to bond with others.

In case you're missing my drift, I'll spell it out. *Our sexual longings are symptoms of our longing for God.* Paul says as much in Ephesians 5, where he describes husband-wife relations. We get so caught up in the sexist implications of Paul's words here that we miss the *sexual* implications of them. He says husbands and wives should submit to, sacrifice for, and care for each other in the same way as Christ and His church do. Then he says the union of husband and wife is the best analogy we have for the God-human relationship.

Did you hear that? *The oneness between husband and wife, which cannot occur without sexual bonding, is the best illustration we have of the divine-human relationship!*

Sex and Commitment

Great sex requires commitment. One of the biggest lies of the sexual revolution is that great sex requires variety and freedom from permanent entanglements. Sex without the hard work of caring, growing, and giving is lite-beer sex—it may taste great, but it's less filling.

Almost every religious writer takes a shot at the *Playboy* philosophy. I'm not interested in adding to the barrage except to say that they usually shoot at the wrong things.

I'm not so much offended by *Playboy*'s photos, or its promotion of "sport sex." That's fantasy stuff. It doesn't take long for the people who try it to leave it. Most guys who look at *Playboy* are like kids watching cops-and-robbers movies. They know the blood and gore aren't real.

My shot at Hefner Inc. has to do with his cheap concept of play. Real, red-blooded, lusty, sexy play can't be done with strangers. Their idea of play is about as real as the sultry looks on the faces of the centerfold models!

Any kind of play that brings joy and is noncompetitive requires that the players not be strangers. Maybe that's why in this age of noncommitment Americans find little joy in sports that are not competitive.

But that's another story. My point is that great sex means the kind of mutual submission, sacrifice, and love modeled by Christ and His church (Eph. 5, again).

Is sex for marriage only? I confess. I searched for a permissive Christian sex ethic for years. (Not in practice, in theory!) Given the changing attitudes toward sex, the prolonged period of adolescence, birth control, and the disproportionate number of women to men, I had to question whether the traditional Christian sex ethic was worth defending anymore.

I dived into personalist ethics, which holds that casual sex in any form is wrong because it violates personhood. And Jesus had the utmost regard for people. Any violation of personality was a sacrilege for him. However, because of the tremendous changes in the world, we must recognize that people can fulfill themselves sexually outside of traditional marriage. The important thing is that sex partners be healthy, independent people who mutually respect each other.

This idea was appealing to me because it upheld personhood and mentioned Christian values. Not only that, it allowed me to ignore all of the foolin' around, livin' with, and shackin' up that was going on around me.

The only problem with personalism is that it's nonsense. In the first place, there's no such thing as a "person" in isolation. To be a person you have to relate to another. The personalists are saying two humans can have sex and remain independent entities at the same time.

Also, Jesus and the personalists don't mean the same thing when they use the same words. For Jesus, "love" meant pouring oneself out for others, not using sex as an instrument to fulfill my personhood.

Great sex is for marriage. But I don't define marriage merely as a legal institution. It's a union based upon mutual lifelong commitment. The only reason for the legal part is to divide up the loot in case of divorce, or to give the kids a name and an inheritance.

But I'm not offering a loophole for sexual commitment. So-called free sex can't last very long. Not for the individual. Not for a society. How many healthy, happy people do you know who play musical beds? How many healthy societies?

What does it take to have a society? Well, people have to surrender some of their individual rights for the good of the whole. They have to agree to certain rules that govern "social transactions," as the pros call them. The basic social transactions are: sex, money, power, and language.

If we don't abide by the rules that govern our monetary transactions, the economy breaks down. If we don't abide by the rules of language, communication breaks down. If we don't abide by political rules, the government breaks down. And if there are no rules governing our sexual transactions, the social structure breaks down.

So, the reason great sex requires commitment is not because I say so. And not even because the Bible says so. But because our human nature says so. It is not natural to be alone, but neither is it natural to be uncommitted

Great Sex and Forgiveness

Sexual betrayal is a big deal with us. We find sexual sins the hardest to forgive. A Christian can gossip, gloat over another's misfortune, backbite, verbally abuse his or her family, and be as mean as a biting sow, and never be called to task.

But let that same Christian get involved with elicit sex and it's all over. Nathaniel Hawthorne's *Scarlet Letter* was all about that. Today things aren't much different from his Puritan world. The scarlet letter's still an "A."

But, in the Bible, sexual sins are no different than any other sin. Sex mess-ups are processed and forgiven. Just look: Lot's incest, David's adultery, Rahab the harlot, and Hosea's wife who sold herself into prostitution—they all recovered and were useful to God's purpose.

And in the New Testament there was Mary Magdalene, the woman at the well, and the adulteress Jesus told to go forth and sin no more. He even said that prostitutes might make it into heaven before the hypocritical Pharisees—the preachers!

Now, I'm not putting in a good word for "foolin' around," I'm just saying that God finds sexual sins easy to erase. That's because he sees our sexual longings for what they are: thrashing about in the thickets of loneliness, searching for at-one-ness. They are also self-centered and destructive.

I'm also saying there can be great sex after we've blown it. The purpose of this piece is to help us reconnect our sexuality to our spirituality. The place to start is with God's forgiveness.

Forgiveness is the route to true morality. The only good that's worth anything is the good we do out of gratitude for having been given a new life. The threat of punishment is the route to resentment. Morality is the freedom to want to do good. Moralism is the fear of doing bad.

Great sex is what God wants for us. People who are struggling with shabby sex lives don't need sermons. They need fellow strugglers. They also need to hear the good news about God's gift of sexuality.

In our church we have Twelve-Step recovery groups for many maladies, including alcoholism, overeating, and drug abuse. I think we need to add three more: *Lovers*

Anonymous, for those who've settled for second-rate sex lives; *Adulterers Anonymous,* for those who have sinned sexually; and *Pharisees Anonymous,* for those who think they haven't.

Chapter 18

KIDS ARE SEXUAL, TOO

Children are sexual when they exit the womb, and they start receiving sex education at the same time. Yet I find very little in Christian literature on how to prepare kids for wholesome sexual experiences later in life.

Sexologist John Money says each of us has a "love-map." It's what we need to get turned on sexually. And our love-map is finished by the age of eight.

If he's anywhere near correct, we're a tad late when we give a ten- or twelve-year-old a "sexplanation manual" and call it sex education.

Is there such a thing as Christian sex education for kids? How do we teach it? What's the material? If you're looking for a biblical text, I don't have one. But I do have a couple of general statements based on a biblical model. First the statements, then the model.

Statement: *Early on, sex is caught, not taught.* Like I said, children are born sexual beings and start learning about sex from the day they're born. Signals are received and stored to be retrieved throughout their lives. By age three, gender roles (who I am), self-worth (how I am welcomed here), and body sense (the value of my body as good or bad) are well into formation.

This is all transmitted by how the baby is cuddled and kept and loved, and by the emotional stability of the care-givers. Even the reaction of the diaper-changer to the diaper sends clear signals about "What's down there below my waist and how should I feel about it?"

The goal is to communicate intimacy, which simply means: *You're welcome, you're loved,* and *you're safe.* If the child doesn't "catch" the signals—that is, if the child misses out on intimacy—the chances are that he or she will try to make up for it with sexual encounters, beginning in adolescence and continuing through the middle-age crazies.

Statement: *Later on, sex is intimated, not demonstrated.* There are two ways to communicate: intimately or demonstratively, that is, with an air of confidence, calm, and safety or with an air of anxiety, threat, and brashness.

When my daughter was eight years old, she came home after school with an "outrageous story" about how babies were made. A classmate had described the process in graphic detail. And as it turned out, the details were outrageously accurate.

"That's not how it's done, is it Dad?" she said. "Yep," I replied, making sure I didn't blink, fidget, or gulp.

You know the next question. "Is that how I was made, Dad?" "Yep." "You mean, you and Mommie...?" I nodded like I was revealing the most wonderful secret in the world.

"Yuck!" said she. "Not yuck later," said I. "I want you to know that you came out of a great love that I can't explain to you because you'll have to experience it for yourself someday. And if God lets Mom and me live to be old, I want to have a family reunion with you and your husband and your kids and their kids. And I want to stand right in the middle of all of you, pat your mom and say, 'Look what love came to!'"

That's intimation. The best way to prepare kids for wholesome sex is to let them know something great's going on between their parents.

Now here's demonstration: I asked my mom how babies were made. The body language was loud and clear. Then she called for Dad—in that quiet way, like in the middle of the night, when we say, "I think someone's in the house."

"What?" said Dad. When he found out, he said, "Come to the study with me." We never sat in the study to talk unless it was grave. He was sweating. It was December. "Do you know what gettin' knocked up means?" I didn't, but I knew that I'd better, so I nodded. "Well, that's what you'll be able to do to a girl pretty soon."

The rest you can guess. He showed me condoms and talked about "the clap" and "the pox." Girls would probably keep me pure, but if they didn't, it was my job to be safe and sanitary.

We never spoke of it again. I took his instruction to school and contributed it to the ignorance pool shared by me and my friends. The only adult information received afterward was the coach telling us not to masturbate before the big game.

Knowing About It

My parents were only teaching what they'd been taught. They had made it through childhood and adolescence with such nonsense, so they figured we could, too. But their main concern was that if we knew about the joys of sex, we'd be stimulated to try it early and often. Knowing about it would lead to doing it.

Just the opposite is true. When kids see their parents go into shock and start talking nonsense about something as mysterious as sex, they're surefire candidates for all-out experimentation. But if they know something first-rate is going on between Mom and Dad, and the folks let the kids in on it—and urge them to look forward to it—the kids aren't likely to settle for something second-rate.

Biblical Sex Education Model

The sex ed. model for kids in the Bible is the kind of family I've already described. You can find it in Ephesians 5 and 6 and in several other places. It's the family that treats each other like Christ and the church treat each other—mutual respect, mutual submission, and mutual sacrifice.

Submission needn't frighten you. It simply means that I cannot act strictly in my own self-interest. Respect simply means recognizing that no child or mate is an extension of me. They have a right to be, so let them be. Sacrifice means pouring myself into another self so that we both grow. If there's no mutual growth, there's no love.

A child who grows up in an atmosphere like that will have a great sex education. The fantasy garbage that's dumped by the world outside may dirty him or her a bit, but the dirt will wash off.

Chapter 19

TEENAGERS: PEOPLE GOD DIDN'T CREATE

I read every authority on adolescence I could find before my first two kids reached puberty. And I preached everything I read. I ran the gamut from old-fashioned whop-'em-and-stop-'em to reasoning with the child. Then they reached puberty, and I preached on other things until they were twenty-one.

Our third child was a belated surprise. We were older and tireder, so we just said "yes" every chance we got and kissed him all we could. We figured we might as well enjoy him before his mutation into monsterhood.

Our kids are all grown now. Thankfully we all survived in one piece. I could share many insights received through those years, but I want to tell you the best thing I've learned about teenagers and what I think it means for parents and kids: *God didn't create them, we did.*

You may have discovered this yourself the hard way, as I did and as others have. In fact, there's a Lutheran minister, Charles Mueller, who wrote an excellent book entitled *Thank God I Have a Teenager.* He has nurtured many of the seeds that grow on these pages.

Let me explain what I mean when I say God didn't create them, we did. We see life in six stages: birth, child, teen, adult, elderly, death. But the Bible sees life in four: birth, child, adult, death. The Bible doesn't even mention adolescence as a stage of life.

God sees teenagers as adults and includes them as part of his redemptive drama. Joseph, David, Daniel, and John were all teenagers who did great things for God. But we don't see it this way. We have created an artificial life-stage that simply doesn't exist in the Bible. The only thing that differentiates a teenager from an adult, as far as God is concerned, is that the teenager has two things called *parents*.

I am convinced that the root of most of our conflict with teenagers is our refusal to see them as God does—as young adults. We see them as "tween-agers," neither fish nor fowl, whom we must mollify, curb, rein in, fear, and hope not to be embarrassed by until they (please God!) leave home.

Okay, that's what I've learned about teenagers—they're adults, except they have parents. Now what does this mean for parents and kids?

Read This

You remember the story: Jesus is twelve years old. His parents are going to the Passover festival in Jerusalem. This time they're taking Him, which means that He's now to be seen as an adult. It's the equivalent of His bar mitzva. After the festival, they start back home and it's not until afternoon that they discover He's missing.

They rush back to Jerusalem. On the third day they find Him in the Temple talking to the teachers. His mother does a typical "I-could-wring-your-neck-but-thank-God-you're-okay-why-did you-do-this-to-me!"

Jesus, in today's language, speaks right back, "Chill out, Mom. I'm where I'm supposed to be. Why did it take you so long to figure out where I was? And what are you doing here anyway?"

Then the story ends saying that Jesus went on home and was obedient to His parents. And we're told that He grew in wisdom, in stature, in favor with God, and in favor with people. That's Luke 2:41-52. And it gives clues to what being a teenager means for parents and kids.

Let Go and Lead

Jesus' parent's task was to let go of Jesus as "child." He wasn't smarting-off to her. In so many words He was saying, "You brought me here as a sign that I'm an adult. Stop treating me like I'm not."

But then it turns around and says Jesus went home and obeyed His parents throughout His teenage years. The word "obeyed" means "was led." He had learned all there was to learn about being a child from them. Now He let them teach Him about being an adult.

Five Rs of Leadership

I made up what I call the five Rs of parental leadership so that I could recite them to myself. Here's what leading a teenager means:

Remembering: If you want to lead a teenager, remember how it felt to be one. Most of us block out that part of our past, but if we try, we can remember how lonely we were, how desperately we wanted to belong, how we hated some part of the way we looked, how scary and sensational our sexual awakenings were, how we liked to poke fun at Dad and hated for him to reciprocate.

Rooting: All kids need somebody in their corner, rooting for them. They need a cheering section most after they've really blown it—after the referee says "you're out" and the crowd is leaving—when she's pregnant, when he's wall-to-wall acne, when first-love (what you see as puppy love) fades.

I heard a mom at the track meet the other day. The event was the 800 meters—twice around the track—for seventh graders! The race had been over for three minutes but here came Buddy, staggering toward the finish line, giving it everything he had.

And Mom put everybody in the stands quiet with her shouting, "Come on, Buddy! Run, Baby! Run!" Teens need parents who root for them.

Respecting: If God sees them as adults, leading has to mean treating them as we do our best friends. When's the last time you told your best friend that he ought to do something about his scuffed shoes or an unwashed pimple? Or his hair? Or his clothes? Or the way he keeps his room? You don't talk to friends that way. That's why they're friends.

Relating: That's a buzzword, but I use it because it starts with R. Relating means talking. I should say talking *with,* not talking *to.* It means talking about things a teenager likes—music, movies, sports. It means asking his or her advice and opinion.

Relaxing: This is my favorite R of parental leadership. Here's how it works for me. My teenager is not mine; he or she is God's. About 90 percent of all teenagers eventually turn out okay in spite of their parents. They are probably more moral than I was because they're exposed to more temptation in a week than I was in eight years. And they seem to hold up just fine.

I'm not in charge of doing anything but leading and modeling. So I relax. That was Jesus' word to Mary and to us. You don't have to be God.

Grab Hold and Grow

Just like all teenagers, though, Jesus' job was to grab hold and grow. He had to grab onto His destiny. He had to pick up what had been laid down. From the moment of His exit from childhood He could no longer blame who or what or how on His folks.

The other part of His task was to grow. And the Bible says He grew in four areas.

Wisdom: Jesus grew in "smarts." He learned things— school things, a trade, order, self-discipline, the laws of cause and effect. He learned how to step outside of Himself and look at Himself. The big word for that is "objectivity." Book smart, street smart, self-smart. The teachers at the Temple were astonished at what He knew. A teenager not wising up is drying up.

Stature: Teenagers grow physically. They need to know what's happening to them *a long time before it starts happening.* Every year thousands of teenage girls think they're bleeding to death when their first period begins. And thousands of boys are horrified by nocturnal emissions. And no one tells them that, simply because they're teenagers, their emotions are accentuated. Their highs are higher and their lows are lower than at any other time of their lives.

And there are parents who still don't know why Junior stops bouncing out of bed when he reaches thirteen. It's not because he's lazy or rebellious or asserting his independence. He just requires more sleep. Chill out, Dad!

With God: Jesus knew God. He knew Him as a friend. And He knew that His dad wasn't His Father, and that His mom wasn't either. And He knew that His Father wasn't His mom or His dad.

I'm not trying to be cute with words. To grow in favor with God is to be able to separate your God-image from your parent-image. Freud was right about some things, and one is that children can't grow unless they are able to distinguish between earth-parent and heaven-parent. There are a lot of fifty-year-olds walking around who don't know their dad from their Father.

Being on speaking terms with God is indispensable for growth. Every human fixation and arrested behavior I've seen in adults over the past thirty years has had something to do with an arrested relationship with the Father.

The key phrase in Jesus' dialogue with His mother is when He asks why they are looking for Him. After all, didn't they know He would be in His Father's house?" (Luke 2:49).

He was saying, *God is my Father. You are my parents.* How do teenagers make it without that kind of growth? They make it painfully or not at all.

With people: The fourth area of growth for Jesus was "in favor with people." Jesus learned how to get on with people. He knew how they thought and felt. He anticipated their moves. He could see His disciples huddled and whispering, and He knew what they were talking about.

For years, I thought He had this uncanny ability to read people because He was God's Son. I don't believe that now. I think Jesus got on so well with people because He learned how to do it. He grew into it as a teenager.

And He shared the secret of how to do it. In eleven words He gave us the formula for "making friends and influencing people": "Do unto others as you would have them do unto you." Now wait! Don't yawn. Think about it. Especially if you are a teenager, or have one, or were one, or may have one someday.

All teenagers are alike in certain ways. They want to be accepted. They're afraid they won't be. They've fallen into what James Dobson calls the "canyon of inferiority." Sarcasm, shyness, loudness, fighting, giggling, conforming dress, hair, language, and music—all of these are their cries to be liked.

People who reach people are the ones who are wise enough to do for others exactly what they'd like to have done to themselves. Figure out your needs. Bet on it—your friends have the same ones. Then meet those needs in others. That's all the lessons you'll ever need on socializing.

And Now for Sex

A teenager's sexual life will be a spin-off of his growth in the four areas I've been talking about. If he's treated as a young adult by parents who have something good cooking between themselves, he'll handle his sexual awakening and development okay.

But I do want to echo what Charles Mueller says. *The primary need of a teenager is not sexual but social.*

Sexual awakening is social awakening. Boys and girls suddenly want to relate to the opposite sex, but they don't know how. I have personally surveyed hundreds of young people in the past five years and asked them to list in order of importance what they want to know about dating.

Their number one concern is, "How do I talk with a girl/boy?" Their curiosity about each other is more than sexual. They're not asking, "How do I get in a girl's pants?" (or "How do I get a boy into mine?"). As Mueller says, "They are yearning to discover what it means to be persons. They believe the best way to discover personness in themselves is to discover the personness in someone else. They are right."[5]

The bottom line is that kids who do not know how to be socially successful will make up for it by being sexually successful. Many sexual encounters happen when teenagers have nothing else to say or do.

Recap

So, I believe we can best help teenagers by starting where God does—by treating them as adults. They are His. We are their mentors and models. Our task is to let go and lead. Theirs is to grab hold and grow.

But what if the gate's been left open at your house, and all of the cows have already gotten out? You haven't let go and led, and your teen hasn't grabbed hold and grown?

Well, let me confess what I hinted at earlier. I learned all of this "great stuff" by messing up two great kids. I didn't let go. I just learned how to tie more umbilical knots. I controlled; they rebelled. It finally got so bad that I wanted to let them go—so far away that I'd never see them again. But they wouldn't leave. They didn't want abandonment. They wanted a leader. That's when I did what we always have to do. I confessed to God and then to them. We cried and started over.

I have to finish this chapter. My grandchild's coming

over this evening. Her mom and dad are having their weekly date away from the kids. My other daughter and her husband are coming from out of town. They only have a few hours. He's attending a law conference and she's giving a paper on relating to kids with learning disabilities.

And I have to go to my son's track meet. He's running the 800 meters. His mom and I are always there to cheer him down the last straightway. Most of the time we're the only ones who are still yelling when he comes around the curve. But lately I've been hearing another voice. Her name's Michelle. They talk a lot.

Chapter 20

AMERICA! AMERICA?
A QUESTION OF COURAGE

Is America a cut-flower culture? Have her roots been severed? Is she only waiting for the stalk to dry out? Or is she simply coming of age? Is she the unruly adolescent of the West who has now matured to the point of becoming one of the family?

Is it, "America!" Or is it, "America?"

From one perspective, it looks like America with the question mark. Technologically, we haven't done very much very well since the lunar landings. Economically, we're now the world's greatest debtor nation. Americans are credit junkies, and we now provide services instead of goods to the world.

Politically the country often seems in disarray. Our politicians call each other names, and our citizens have a hard time getting up the enthusiasm to exercise their right to vote.

The litany of our ills is endless. But the fact is, *there's not one thing wrong with America that can't be cured.*

I'm neither optimistic nor pessimistic about the country's future. It's up for grabs. Everything depends on two things: (1) an understanding of how we really got here; and (2) whether we have the courage to deal with what went wrong.

How Did We Get Here?

How did America rise to prominence? Some have said it's because of her vast natural resources, or her safe location between two oceans, or her economic-political structure, or her accident of birth just before the Age of Industrialization, or her strategic time of entry into the two great wars—or all of the above. Others say we got where we are by accident. Some say we got here because we had great leaders. (If they're right, we're in big trouble now!)

Let me venture another opinion. I think civilizations are born and energized out of great ideas, central driving notions—which are really decisions about reality—that catch on and are put into practice.

To find the basic idea that brought America to power, you have to go back several thousand years to the moment when somebody decided to live by a new idea. The idea was to stop trying to escape from the material world and dive into it instead.

Before this decision, people saw the material world as evil. The human self was imprisoned in an evil body. History went in a circle, repeating itself without alteration. The key to human meaning was to escape matter and get off the wheel of time by means of a series of reincarnations. The ultimate goal was to escape individuality and be absorbed into the universal soul. Suffering was the result of one's attempt to be an individual material entity.

The result was a society of rigid castes where no one attempted to "make history." By obeying the rules of the caste, one could "move up" toward nonexistence as an individual material entity. This is a gross simplification, but the point is that fulfillment was sought through escape from matter.

Then someone made a radical decision that caught on. It shows up in ancient Hebrew thought as a revelation from God. It separates East from West.

The decision was that matter was good, not evil—literally, *that matter mattered!* The material world was a gift to humans. They were to use it to fulfill themselves.

God is in the world, not outside of it. Time is linear, not cyclical. Meaning is formed by managing and using nature's bounty. Individuals count here and hereafter. This radical decision made possible all of the things that many writers identify as the source of America's greatness.

Exploration of the New World, synchronization of time, individual liberty, industrialization—these didn't make America great. They are the *result* of what made America great, namely the idea that matter is good and usable for human fulfillment.

In this sense, America is not great because she's rich. She's rich because she's great. We are the bloom on the stalk whose seed was the decision to use nature's bounty.

And this seed is also the seed of biblical religion. The world is the product of God's joy to create. Matter and time are the places where God meets people. He met them face to face in *matter,* in the flesh of Jesus the Christ, the perfect union of matter and spirit.

You're right. I went all the way around the horn to come back and say that what got us here is the basic idea of the Judeo-Christian worldview. Without it there would be no capitalism, no development of nature's treasures, no Bill of Rights.

The Two Choices of Materialism

The decision to get involved with the material world creates two choices for humans. We can either drown in it or use it. We can be owners or tenants.

If we decide to own nature's bounty, we lose our link to God. Only if we see ourselves as tenants, cultivators, multipliers, managers of property placed in our care by the Creator, does matter become the means of blessing ourselves and others.

That's what the Adam-and-Eve-in-the-Garden story is about. Adam and Eve are tenants in the Garden. The forbidden tree is there to remind them they are not the owners. The reason they will "die" if they eat from the tree is because they will "drown in matter"; they will lose their spiritual link.

The founding fathers understood this choice well. And they practiced tenancy perhaps better than any group before them. They were able to balance their material prosperity with spiritual discipline.

The economic and political applications of their central driving idea appeared in the capitalism of Adam Smith and the political philosophy of Thomas Jefferson, *et al.* Smith's economics centered in the notion that an "unseen hand" worked to the good of all concerned when individual transactions were free of interference from government.

Jefferson and his cohorts did not profess "Christianity," but they were used by its underlying notion. They understood that whether it rested in the hands of the state or the individual, power inured to evil and needed to be held in check. They guaranteed to the *individual* the inalienable right to life, liberty, and the pursuit of material fulfillment, but within the larger context of the "common good."

So America didn't just happen. It rose on the tide of a great notion. And it kept its soul by choosing tenancy instead of ownership. Our forefathers saw themselves as "called" by God to dive into the world and make it a better place. They made the first choice of materialism: to use things and enjoy people.

Another way to say this is that they achieved a healthy balance between *individual rights* and the *common good.* When individuals are left to themselves to find fulfillment, they will do so at the expense of others. That's what makes power the culprit. The good of the whole has to check individual rights. The self with its things is an "individual." The self with other selves is a "person." The decision to use things for the common good as well as individual enhancement was the most significant choice of the founding fathers.

The Wrong Choice

But somewhere along the way enough people who made a difference started making the "second choice of materialism": to *use people and enjoy things.* America is now obsessed with owning instead of tending.... We have cut our link to the "blessing part" of material prosperity. Literally, we have gained the whole world but lost our souls. We have drowned in our "stuff."

Our problem is of the spirit. We haven't lost our drive to wrest away nature's bounty, but we have lost our means for enjoying it. The self is now "the individual"—the self with its things.

This choice to separate our things from our God shows itself mostly in the loss of a national courage or will. We are unable to unite and sacrifice against common enemies at home or abroad. We have enthroned the individual at the expense of the common good. We are selves with things, not selves with other selves.

Alexander Solzhenitsyn, the former Russian exile and Nobel laureate, has spoken often of the decline of courage in the West. He's spoken so candidly that we like to ignore him. He says that we have bought into the notion that we humans are the crowning glory of the universe, with no Supreme Being above us. From that assumption, the outcome is inevitable. *Personal material satisfaction becomes the supreme moral authority.* Everything is judged by whether it betters or preserves our economic well-being.

The end result is a loss of courage to be motivated by anything but economic considerations. Unless it threatens our pocketbooks, we don't get involved!

Solzhenitsyn's popularity on the speaking circuit has waned since the middle 1970s. We always tend to ignore "prophets who threaten profits." What he was saying to us back then needs saying again. Here's a sample:

> It is with a strange feeling that those of us who come from the Soviet Union look upon the West of today... *We see our past repeating itself.* It is the same here as it was there: Adults deferring to the opinions of their children; the younger generation being carried away by worthless ideas and professors scared of being unfashionable; journalists refusing to take responsibility for the words they squander so easily... people with serious objections unable or unwilling to voice them; feeble governments; societies whose defensive reactions have become paralyzed.[6]

A Question of Courage

I have read and reread Solzhenitsyn's words often. We have a future that can bless the whole planet—if we have the courage to recover our spiritual center. The sobering fact is, I cannot think of a nation that has ever done it successfully. But that doesn't mean it can't be done.

There are hopeful signs. Americans are coming back to church in record numbers. Beginning with Jimmy Carter's anti-Washington campaign in 1976, the American people have consistently voted in the direction of "traditional values." The "big story" about religion in the past two decades was not the Moral Majority, televangelists, and so forth. It was the untold story of the return to spirituality by everyday folk.

A national political media consultant tells me that he's done a revealing profile on so-called Yuppies. He says Yuppies are as compassionate as any generation in history, but they refuse to be intimidated by purveyors of guilt.

They work seventy hours a week, they've paid the price of an education; and they're interested in a home, kids, and the neighborhood. They are willing to help people help themselves, but they refuse to reinforce sloth and corruption by supporting federal handouts.

These are hopeful signs of spiritual renewal, but it's too early to tell whether they will translate into a national courage that is strong enough to face up to the issues that face us. Keep in mind that the issue underlying all of the issues that threaten our social fabric is the courage to say "no" to the imperial self and "yes" to the common good...to reject the "self with its things" and to embrace the "self with other selves."

Psychology professor Dr. Martin Seligman spoke of this in a speech to the American Psychological Association in 1988. In addressing why the national rate of emotional and mental depression has increased tenfold in forty years, he said the individual self has been stripped of the support system that used to be there when we failed—faith in God, faith in country, and faith in family.

When all we have to depend on is ourselves, we are doomed to inevitable depression.

> One necessary condition for finding meaning in our lives is an attachment to something larger than the lonely self. To the extent that young people now find it hard to take seriously their relationship with God, to care about their relationship with the country, or to be a part of a large and abiding family, they will find it very difficult to find meaning in life. To put it another way, the self is a very poor site for finding meaning.[7]

So the real question facing our culture is this: Do we have the courage to correct this rampant idolatry of the self with a commitment to the common good? Our future depends on the answer.

Chapter 21

CALLS TO COURAGE

It's one thing to talk about the need for a spiritual center that translates into a national courage or will. But what does this courage look like when it comes to living real life, the issues we face every day? How do we keep our spiritual center and actually make the tough choices that the politicians are always crowing about? Here are several issues that call us to courage as a society.

When Susie Says She's Gay

Your sermon was just what we didn't need. Three years ago our daughter told us she thought she might be gay. Several counselors, psychiatrists, and preachers later, she moved out. The gay world is a kingdom unto itself. We lost track of her for months at a time. Her comrades could undo in an hour what it took us months to tie together.

She finally came home for Easter. She's always liked you, so we got her to church. Then you did your X-rated garbage about God's forgiveness. Where in the Bible do you find that the only hell there is, is the one we make for ourselves? You just killed our only chance to get our daughter back. You gave her the license she needed to keep doing what she's been doing.

This letter came from a friend. He was hurt bad, and that's why he was snarling at me. He knew my sermon didn't topple his world; it had crumbled long before. He knew I knew his pain. So, when I called on him, we wept together.

We knew the real question: How could he relate to his Susie now that he knew she was gay? Not, "What is the official Christian position on homosexuality?" That would have been easy enough. He didn't need a position paper; he needed a position!

The torment of this father is the torment of the church. The Bible may be unrelenting about the "sin of homosexuality," but that doesn't erase the existence of homosexuals.

How are we Christians to relate to the real people we know who are gay? Of course, if we believe that homosexuality erases the God-image and places all gays beyond the pale, then we don't have to ask the question. We can trash and bash—even in the name of God!

As for myself, I must ask the question for one simple reason: No one is beyond the grace of God unless he or she chooses to be, otherwise God would not be gracious. And I never heard or read of a homosexual who chose to be one!

Notwithstanding recent claims that homosexuality is genetic, the best data we have suggests that every child is born with the potential to develop either way sexually. Something happens during early development to seal sexual identity. People don't choose to be gay.

Point: If a person doesn't choose to become gay, how can he or she be blamed for being so? How could God condemn this person? So I *have* to face the question of how to relate to gay people.

I start by admitting that I have a built-in, gut-level revulsion to the very thought of homosexuality, and I'm convinced this is not a *learned* prejudice. No one had to teach my skin to crawl at the very notion of homosexuality. It was woven into the fabric of my existence. It was primordial. It's not unlike the feeling I had when first I saw a snake.

I think many heterosexuals have this basic reaction to homosexuality. I'm not justifying it. I'm simply admitting to it and describing it. I think the biblical writers shared the same revulsion. For them, homosexuality was basically unnatural. It was against nature and therefore against God. Also I believe this is the key to understanding the primordial revulsion which we straights experience.

To begin with, if everyone were gay, the human race would become extinct! To reject reproduction is to reject one's own gene pool. It is cross-current to millions of years of genetic survival. It is unnatural in the sense that it is against the entire evolution of one's race. It is a saying-no to one's own ancestry and progeny. It is the ultimate rebellion against one's own life.

No wonder straights have a knee-jerk reaction to gays! The gay community finds this attitude cruel. They protest it. Nevertheless, it is there, and it is unavoidable. No amount of propaganda will erase it.

As a Christian, I cannot begin to relate to a homosexual until I get in touch with this primordial revulsion. I just have to admit that gays are perceived at the gut level as a threat to my existence.

On the other side of the equation are gay people themselves. They possess all of the love and relational needs of any human. Such people are enraged by the idea of being in any way "other" and liken the sexual difference to nothing more than being left-handed .

So the battle lines are drawn. On the one side the heterosexual, with millions of years of conditioned defenses;

on the other side the homosexual, who feels persecuted.

If my first task is to understand and accept the conflict, the second is to decide how to relate, given this conflict. The Bible is rather clear on the subject. The Old Testament writers follow their pattern of having God curse anything that hinders the procreation of the race. But in the New Testament, Paul suggests that confused sexual identity goes hand in hand with confused human identity. When humans start worshipping the created order instead of the One who created it, they also get mixed up about their being in general and their sexuality in particular (Rom. 1:18-32).

In the same passage, however, Paul also includes envy, murder, strife, lying, adultery, bragging, and gossip to the list of human confusions resulting from our separation from God. A person couldn't run for president if we took away the freedom to practice most of these!

In view of everything I've said so far, here is how I have chosen to relate to the homosexuals I know. Up front, I confess the bias I have described. I don't apologize for it; I simply admit to it. Then I tell them that I view homosexuality as a deep-seated psychological confusion, a more serious malady than being left-handed. It is learned behavior and can be unlearned. I do not accept homosexual practice as a "legitimate alternative lifestyle." It is an aberration, a bump in the road of the natural order. It is an exception that would bring about human extinction if it became the rule.

I am not alone in these opinions, nor are they "merely opinions." Leanne Payne, Ruth Barnhouse, Agnes Sanford, Dr. Frank Lake, and others concur. They have treated homosexuals successfully and seen them resume normal heterosexual lives. Payne's book, *The Broken Image,* is a documented case study I highly recommend.

A disease is not a crime. Gays should not be incriminated unless they commit crimes, just as manic depressives shouldn't be locked up for being depressed.

When I am asked if homosexuality is a sin, I really get tongue-tied. The answer is "Yes, but ..." I agree with Paul that homosexuality is the result of God's creation gone wrong—"fallout from the Fall." In this sense, yes, homosexual behavior is against God's purpose for creation and therefore sinful.

But sinful behavior should not be a cause for banishment from society or church unless it poses a danger to the community as a whole. In other words, homosexuality is as forgivable as any of the sins on Paul's list.

I tell homosexuals they are welcome in my world and in my church (*along with myself and all of the other sinners*). But don't confuse acceptance with endorsement. No one can remain part of a family or a church body if he or she flaunts destructive behavior and refuses to begin becoming whole. (Paul instructed the church at Corinth to dismiss a man who was flaunting a sexual affair with his stepmother.)

There is an entirely different option for Christian homosexuals, and it is being lost in the midst of the civil rights–gay rights rhetoric. C. S. Lewis mentioned it years ago in a letter to a friend. Lewis noted that many humans have different kinds of disabilities that deprive them of living as fully as others. The deaf, the blind, the paraplegic are all restricted. A poor man does not have as many options as a rich one. But Lewis insists that *every disability conceals a vocation*. A disability can either use us, or be used by us to fulfill a mission no one else can. So it is for the homosexual! The privation can be accepted as an opportunity to fulfill missions under God that others cannot.

So Susie is welcome to come home and be part of the family. She is not welcome to impose her illness on the family. She can expect to be loved and accepted as a fellow sinner but she cannot expect her sexual preference to be blessed. Nor can she expect me to feel guilty because I have a "natural resistance" to her lifestyle. The fact is that Susie and I must accept the tension that will always exist between us.

If she chooses to practice her homosexuality, she and I will have to struggle in that cold gray area of acceptance without endorsement. If she seeks healing, she can count on my support. Otherwise, a passable truce may be the best that we two sinners can achieve.

I cannot banish her from my table and we cannot eat our bread with gladness. We both need grace and courage. God help us.

Abortion: After the Myths

If you're going to frame a Christian response to abortion, you must first whittle your way through the myths. For example, there's the myth that abortion is not killing. No one would argue that terminating a child outside the womb is killing, but all kinds of chatter arise when we discuss terminating it prior to exit. Obviously, abortion is killing! The question is whether there are ever any circumstances that justify killing.

Then there's the myth that a woman has complete right to her body and therefore is free to choose abortion upon demand. Nonsense! A woman has a complete right to her body *until* she invites someone else into it. She has the right not to get pregnant. If we are more than animals and if sex is more than biological recreation, this must be so. Thus abortion is a societal choice as well as an individual one. The question is whether there are ever any circumstances in which individual choices should prevail over societal choices, and vice-versa.

This brings us to the third myth: A law cannot be drafted that is both sensible and enforceable. Again, nonsense! We have had such laws, we do have them, and we can have them. The question is whether we have the courage to legislate abortion.

The fourth myth is that abortions are for anything except convenience. Nearly all abortions are for the sake of convenience. A pregnancy is terminated because it is deemed better to abort than to deliver. The question is whether there are cases where convenience justifies abortion.

The last myth is that abortion makes no imprint upon the human psyche and upon a society's appreciation for life. Humans simply cannot participate in the mystery of procreation and then terminate it without effect. The killing of four thousand fetuses a day must do "something" to us. The question is whether we're willing to tolerate that "something."

Point: We must get past the myths and ask the right questions: Is there ever a situation where killing is justified? As a society, we have said "yes" in other instances where the victims were unable to defend themselves—namely, in war. When we bombed Nagasaki and Hiroshima we knew that thousands of innocent noncombatants would be killed. Killing was deemed justified in view of the alternatives. Also, abortion has long been accepted in cases where a mother's life was at risk.

These kinds of decisions make it clear that there's no such thing as an absolute set of rules that apply to all cases all of the time.

As Reinhold Neibuhr showed us years ago, we are constantly faced with choices between the lesser of two evils rather than between absolute good and evil.

I remember Joseph Fletcher's hypothetical story: A German wife and mother who got caught in the mayhem of World War II ended up in a Russian prison camp. After the war ended, the Russians kept women as forced labor to produce garments. However, they had to release those who became pregnant because of the lack of facilities to care for them. The German woman was a devout Christian and she had a husband and sick child back home. She consorted with a Russian guard to become pregnant, was released, and returned to fulfill her role as wife and mother. And she raised the illegitimate child as one of the family.

Was what she did with the guard wrong? Or was it the least of several wrongs from which she had to choose?

Obviously, an absolute "situational ethic" is ridiculous. You can't change your values with every situation. But an absolute legal ethic won't hold water either. There will always be *extreme* cases where our choices are not black and white. The truth is, we can rant and rave all we like about absolute moral rules, but in actual everyday living, none of us practices strict absolutism.

This brings us back to abortion. Are there cases other than danger to the life of the mother that make killing a fetus the lesser of the evil choices? What about in cases of rape or incest or fetal malformation?

Many would say that abortion is justified in these instances. But where does the list stop? If abortion is both a societal and an individual matter, shall we ever reach total consensus on where the list stops? No, but that is true on other issues as well! We don't ignore stealing because there is widespread disagreement on what constitutes thievery. Instead, we involve as many and as much as we can in formulating a response, and then we delegate the administration of the decision.

My point is that we don't have a problem to solve. We have decisions to make. We must decide whether to allow abortion and under what conditions. Decisions like this are never final because they correspond to our values and to our moral courage at any given time. To dump these decisions off on "individual choice" is to reject our responsibility for each other as a community. To make a blind absolute law is equally irresponsible.

We must have the courage to call abortion what it is and to accept responsibility for it. We must have the courage to call it convenience and decide where convenience becomes an excuse for our flabby, shallow pursuit of comfort. The fact is that the overwhelming majority of abortions in this country are among the population that can economically afford to raise children! The fact is that those who counsel with postabortion patients almost universally agree that indiscriminate abortion must go.

We must have the courage to see that we cannot terminate millions of lives without effect. We must retain the capacity to be amazed at "our incapacity to be amazed" that 1.5 million fetuses are killed annually. We must have the courage to distinguish between unwanted children and unwanted burdens.

For me, abortion is more than a theoretical discussion. My wife was six weeks pregnant with our first child when she contracted rubella. In 1958, abortion was out of the question. Our child was born profoundly deaf.

Our entire adult lives have been influenced by the management of her handicap. Her life has seen much tragedy. Deafness is one of the most misunderstood and least noticed of the handicaps, mainly because it is invisible. Unless you have lived with a deaf person, you cannot begin to identify with the stress and difficulty the malady brings.

For example, in the early years a deaf child commands almost total attention from his or her parents in order to gain the simplest communication skills. Of the twenty-four sets of parents of the children in my daughter's preschool therapy class, only two couples stayed together.

The overwhelming majority of hearing-impaired adults in this country who are self-supporting either have some hearing or they learned to talk before they lost their hearing. The rest for the most part require government assistance of some kind.

Even the most adept lip-readers seldom comprehend more than two-thirds of what is said orally. They must guess at the rest. Simply watching a television program is an ordeal for a family with a deaf member. If you stop and explain the part he or she missed, you miss the part that occurred while you were explaining!

In all honesty, we have wondered at times—knowing what we know now—what we would have done had abortion been an option for us those years ago. Brainless fanatics who rant "pro-life without exception" simply haven't been there.

However, as I write this, I smell the scent of baby lotion on my shirt. My granddaughter, hearing and healthy and pink—this little daughter of my daughter who has already heard more in twenty-nine months than her mother has in twenty-nine years—she is worth it all!

Her mother is happily married and gainfully employed. She is a living testimony to the triumph of the human spirit. She has lived through the mockery of schoolmates; the ill-guided counsel of well-meaning experts; the horrors of doing anything to gain acceptance; the anger of cursing God for not being able to hear; and the immaturity of parents who thought they could shelter her from all of the pain.

The brainless fanatics who rant "pro-choice without exception" haven't been there either!

My point in all of this is that we cannot rest safely in the absolutism on the right or on the left of the abortion issue. My own experience has taught me that I cannot summarily condemn people for aborting a fetus ravaged by a rubella virus. At the same time, I can say without apology that I'm glad I didn't.

Have you seen the commercial that shows a career mother of two rushing to get them fed and off to the baby-sitter so she can make an important business meeting? She tells us why she takes the newest headache remedy: "Because I haven't got time for the pain." Neither did eight thousand procreators today. But they did have time for the pleasure.

This I know for sure. Humans under God can endure all things. For a few, in a few extreme cases, perhaps they should not have to. There must be grace for these. It is easy to play God by judging them for playing God. But there must be grit for the millions of Americans who view pregnancy as a headache and abortion as the tasteless, odorless, fast-acting, pain reliever.

Predators

While sitting in a leopard blind in Africa one evening I wrote the following words in my diary:

> "As the sun sinks over the Luangwa River in northern Zambia, I listen and look. The issues of the African wild are pristinely clear: There are the hunters, the hunted, and the scavengers—predators, prey, and the clean-up crew.
>
> The prey are definitely in the middle. Their entire life process is simplified: to eat and reproduce in between being clawed, crunched, gnawed, fanged, or swallowed. In the wild, few live to a ripe old age, die in their sleep, and are eulogized by their peers. Violent death is simply a matter of when. A drink of water or a munch of grass is never taken tranquilly. Eyes dart constantly. Shadows become monsters instantly.

That's how I saw it in the jungle. That's how some think it's becoming in the city. Bernard Goetz thought it was already that way when he started shooting in the New York subway.

The civilized human world is now unable to control its predators. The public now incarcerates itself—we lock ourselves up from the criminals. We even blame ourselves for creating them! We tell ourselves that they victimize us only because we have victimized them. Punishment of crime has become a crime, according to many.

Everyone knows that our criminal justice system doesn't work. We common folk think we know why, but we're told we're wrong by the experts. So we reserve our opinions for the ears of our fellow serfs who will not laugh at us for revealing the redness of our necks.

Educated ministers like myself dare not suggest that predators are in fact just *that,* and by choice. We prefer the fashionable arguments of theology, sociology, and the editorial page. We are adept at burying the victim of a "senseless crime" over breakfast in the morning and extolling the evils of capital punishment at evening tea.

Academia has three shining flaws: its worship of the new, its desire to be "in," and the need to be benign—that is, old solutions simply won't do for new problems, we must never be laughed "out" of our peer group, and our conclusions must always be benign.

Today's newspaper reports the punishment phase of the trial of a forty-two-year-old murderer-rapist convicted of murdering two coeds twenty-one years ago. After serving twenty years, he met and married a criminologist who managed to get him a new trial. He was promptly reconvicted (the jury was out eleven minutes), and now the judge is hearing testimony from psychiatrists presented respectively by the prosecution and the defense to determine whether the convicted man is still a threat to society.

The psychiatrist who examined him twenty years ago thinks he's no longer dangerous. He says that at the time of the murder the offender had "a sexual fantasy driven by low self-esteem. He was a schizoid personality and should have been admitted to a hospital for the criminally insane."

However, says the psychiatrist, he is no longer a schizoid personality. The reason? Now hear this: *Because the definition of schizoid by the American Psychiatric Association has changed since the murders were committed in 1965!*[8]

A *new* definition of an old malady; an *"in"* diagnosis reaches the *benign* conclusion that the man is cured! And when the prosecutor asks, "Are you telling me that [this murderer] has been cured by the American Psychiatric Association?" the good doctor answers, "In a sense, yes."

Predator control requires some hard decisions. It requires admitting that many of the theories of modern psychodynamic psychology are simply not valid. We have to admit failure. We also have to admit that the only people who are having much success in helping criminals change are using methods "so old, they're new."

Dr. Samuel Yochelson and his student Dr. Stanton Samenow have been successful in habilitating criminals by a radical return to such traditional assumptions as: (1) people are free to choose their behavior; (2) there is a clear difference between good and evil that humans can perceive and act on; (3) humans can overcome temptation; and (4) criminals are responsible for their behavior, society is not.

Their work has convinced them that criminals are not created by their environment nor can they be changed by its alteration. Criminals think differently than noncriminals. They perceive reality in a peculiar way. This fundamental perception pattern must be changed; finding out why a person commits a crime is beside the point. The important thing is for the criminal not to commit crimes. Yochelson and Samenow have devised a treatment system that habilitates many. They believe that those who do not change should be locked away until they do.

What these "pioneers" are saying in the field of criminology is being said by many of their counterparts in other disciplines. The idea that humans will change bad behavior once they understand its causes simply doesn't work.

Knowing why I do something won't make me stop doing it. Statistics show that only two percent of the people who find out the "why" ever change it.

Christians also need to reassess crime and punishment. The clergy is divided. On one extreme are those who have bought into the whole "society's-to-blame" mentality. They call for prison reform and the abolition of the entire concept of punishment, not to mention capital punishment. On the opposite extreme is the "turn-or-burn" crowd. Quoting heavily from the Old Testament, they pronounce wrath on the wrongdoers and those who sympathize with them.

Somewhere in the middle are souls like me. On the one hand I want to heed Jesus' words about taking an eye for an eye and turning the other cheek (Matt. 5:38-39). On the other, I realize that a society which cannot control its predators will eventually be eaten by them.

This means that my position will be a hard one to hold. It's easy to take up a position on the right or the left. There's always plenty of company in both camps. The middle way is the hardest way of all.

The reason it's hard is because it forces me to choose between the lesser of two evils—the evil of the criminal and the evil of his peers who punish him. I cannot forget the historical accounts of families bringing picnic lunches to watch public executions in an atmosphere of glee and festivity. Neither can I forget holding the hand of a dear old saint whose husband of forty years had been bludgeoned to death by two paroled murderers. Their take was forty-seven dollars and a box of pastries!

I'm saying that there is no tidy choice. We live in a broken world. And when it comes to crime and punishment we must do two things. First, reach as high as we can for the ideal. Second, realize that we will have to reach again and again, because we can never reach high enough.

What does this mean in practical terms? It means that criminals should be separated from society until we find an effective way to habilitate them. If the courts keep turning the predators loose, it means that capital punishment has to remain an option. It means that more money has to be spent, but not on more of the same.

I agree with Yochelson and Samenow. "Rehabilitation" is a misnomer. The criminal mind has never been habilitated in the first place.

"Getting tough on crime" doesn't mean an eye for an eye—executing everyone who murders, castrating rapists, or making amputees out of amputators. It means *getting tough on the way we think about crime and criminals*. People commit crimes by choice. Good *versus* evil. People can change the way they think and act. Society has a right to control its predators. Accused predators have the right to prove they aren't, and convicted predators have the right to prove they aren't anymore.

In the final analysis, my task as a Christian is to try to keep the pendulum from swinging to extremes. I must remember that I am not God. I have no authority to "prey on the predators" at will. But I must also remember that I have the God-given responsibility to be part of a surviving social order. At present, the predators are winning.

Uncensored Bridleship

News in America is business. Like auto manufacturing and banking, the news business has been reduced to a few giants who compete by mutually accepted rules for profit. News-Biz is an oligopoly. On TV, newsreaders are called "journalists" and are paid enormous sums according to their ability to *look* believable.

In a free society, News-Biz must be uncensored by the government. But in a free-enterprise society, it must also be uncensored by moral responsibility or it cannot maintain optimum profitability. It must be able to determine freely what "news" is, or it cannot compete. In a word, it must be able to "bridle" its audience with stories that sell. Its greatest fear is unbridled censorship. Its greatest need is "uncensored bridleship."

A polarized society is a moneymaker for News-Biz. That's why extremists garner most of the news. Twenty people who smoke dope and practice free love in the name of Jesus are newsmakers. Two thousand who gather weekly at my church are not.

A few years ago Dr. Carl Sagan appeared on television to debate evangelist James Robison concerning evolution *versus* the Bible. Sagan ruled out any divine activity in creation. Robison called Sagan Satan. No one was there to say the Bible and evolution are compatible. The mediating viewpoint was simply not news.

Low behavior in high places sells. High behavior in low places doesn't. Conspiracy, real or imagined, sells. Fidelity and loyalty don't. Hasty, superficial tidbits sell. In-depth analysis is for PBS.

News-Biz is more powerful than the three branches of American government, and it answers to no one but its own conscience. It can bring down a president or someone who wants to be a president with as little as innuendo and unflattering photography.

Abe Lincoln could not have survived News-Biz. Like Tom Eagleton, George McGovern's short-lived running mate, he had a nervous breakdown in his past. He was gangly and had an unpleasant whine in his speech. Is it coincidental that actors are now big, both in politics and TV journalism?

Can we do anything but complain? Yes, if we have the national will. News reporting must be separated from the demands of commercial success. It must be deprofitized, and people who report the news must meet the same minimum standards as other professionals.

News reporters should be classified as "public figures." The personal moral character of the reporter should be as open to public scrutiny as the lives of the people he or she claims to be telling the truth about. We are entitled to know about the integrity of the reporter's everyday life if we are expected to believe his or her reports.

Beyond this, controlling the press would be more damaging than leaving them be. The American people are not easily misled.

In the end, I think News-Biz is rather like hemorrhoids: a constant irritation. When they come down on you, they're a real pain. But removing them just ain't worth the gaffe.

Tax Deform

Politicians are elected to raise revenues by taxing an electorate who won't reelect them if they do. Since politics is the business of getting and keeping power, politicians have to tax us without our knowing it. I like to call this "tax deform."

There are many kinds of tax deform. Inflation is one. First the government borrows a lot of money. Then it prints money to devalue its debt. Inflation is a debtor-government's best friend.

When the public finally figures out they're being had, the federal policy changes. The politicians point fingers and become righteously indignant. The printing presses are slowed, the national debt ratchets up, and we move to another type of Tax Deform called tax reform.

Have you noticed that every tax reform in our history has also been a tax increase? What the politicians do is find where the money is and deform the system to go after it.

The so-called Tax Reform Act of 1986 brings no additional money into the till. It just taps a different group. The politicians were out of funds, and they had no pluck for raising taxes or cutting programs.

Here's just one example of what they did. First they announced tax exemptions for lower-income citizens, most of whom rent their domiciles. Next, they canceled the deductions of interest and property taxes for the owners of rental property. The landlords will now be forced to raise rents in order to retain their rental properties. So the low-income people who have just been "exempted" from paying income taxes will be helping the landlord pay his!

There are countless other ways we are taxed by the deformers. Some we probably will never know. It's the nature of the political beast. Democrats and Republicans are no different. They'd just as soon milk a donkey as an elephant.

But the solution is not as simple as "throwing the rascals out." The "rascals" are *our* representatives! They reflect *our* values!

"I want Government to handle the difficult problems. I can't feed the bums, let Washington do it. There outta be a law! Why doesn't the government do something? I'm too busy just trying to survive (make payments on two houses, two cars, two vacations, two dentists, and two charities). I don't have time to get involved in politics." These are the attitudes that create tax deform.

But every time I say "the government," I'm saying "me." Real tax reform won't occur until enough of *us* want it too. Actually, income tax reform is quite simple in theory. Exempt the first $15,000 of income, and tax everything else at a flat rate.

Of course, almost all of the IRS employees would be out of work. So would the tax accountants and the tax lawyers. (So far, so good.) Eventually so would everybody who isn't involved in the production of goods and services. And I mean those who actually produce, not those who live off of them.

Real tax reform would lead to real social reform.

Tax deform is really only the child of moral deform. You can't change one without the other.

Acquired Immune Decision Syndrome

An AIDS carrier sold his contaminated blood for eight dollars. When arrested, he said he knew he had AIDS and he was beyond caring. He was dying and he needed eight bucks.

The district attorney charged him. Then an ABC *Nightline* segment was born. The guests were an Ivy League law professor, the D.A., and an attorney who specializes in defending the rights of AIDS victims. With Ted Koppel as referee, they had quite a row.

The lawyer said having AIDS isn't a criminal offense. AIDS victims are desperate and can't be held accountable for their actions. The D.A. said mostly that's true, except being desperate is no excuse for distributing a lethal disease. The professor was characteristically professorial. He held as how both were partially right and partially wrong, and that AIDS carriers who intentionally become AIDS spreaders should be incarcerated in something *between* a jail and a hospital.

All agreed that the AIDS problem was "enormously complex." The show closed with the three guests carping in the background and Koppel doing his TV-super-journalist sign-off.

Acquired Immune Deficiency Syndrome will probably kill millions. Acquired Immune *Decision* Syndrome will definitely kill us all. The AIDS problem is still another example of the enthronement of the individual over the common good. We seem to become paralyzed whenever we have to make decisions that even vaguely relate to moral behavior or lifestyle.

The tough decision is always the one that favors the rights of some over the rights of others. It's the decision that cannot be justified as being totally right for all parties concerned. But no civilization survives once it loses its courage to make such decisions.

The standard procedure for containing an incurable, contagious disease is to identify and quarantine the carrier until a cure can be found. Clearly this procedure is out of the question where AIDS is concerned. Practically speaking, it would drive the carriers underground. But there is another factor. AIDS emanates in part from a certain social behavior, and is therefore the first "civil rights disease" in our history. That's why about all we can do is hand out condoms and talk about safe sex. We dare not speak to the value system and lifestyle that is related to the disease for fear that we might infringe upon someone's constitutional rights.

I was part of a task force charged with studying AIDS and making recommendations to our state legislature concerning potential legislation. I resigned after one meeting because the ethics panel on which I sat was clearly more interested in protecting the anonymity of the AIDS carrier than the health of the public.

It was clear that the "gay rights–civil rights" aspect of the issue was in charge. The panel consisted of a gay clergyman, an ACLU attorney, and myself. To suggest that uninfected people were justified in separating themselves from carriers until more was known about the transmission of the disease was anathema.

All of the medical research we studied had qualifiers like "although," and "might be," and "as far as we can tell," and "suggests," and "up to now."

To wit (my emphasis): *"Up to now* research suggests that the AIDS virus can be transmitted only by the direct exchange of body fluids via sexual intercourse, blood transfusions, and contaminated needles. *Although* a few cases indicate that French kissing *might be* a possible mode of transmission, *as far as we can tell,* there is no major cause for contacting AIDS except in the instances mentioned above."

Since the release of that statement experts have removed the qualifiers and pronounced "French kissing" safe. Many fears have been relieved, but I still have a question.

What is the Christian response to AIDS? You don't have

to guess that I favor the way of the tightrope, which draws fire from all sides. To start with, the *only* solution, the one we cannot lose sight of, is to pour our might into finding a cure.

Christians can have an enormous impact on this effort. First, we can defuse the irrational elements on both sides of the issue. I have ministered to both categories of AIDS victims—the innocent bystander who was infected by a blood transfusion while having a simple surgery, and the "collaborative victim" who endangered himself by having sex with several high-risk partners.

I visited with and buried them both. At a distance, I had compassion only for the "innocent" one. Up close I had compassion for both. It's easy to hate from afar.

We can defuse the fierce condemnation of the righteously indignant. We can also defuse the "bleeding heart" idealism of those who would exonerate spreaders of the disease who want their irresponsible behavior blessed and protected.

Biblical religion has an AIDS prevention program. It's called chastity, fidelity, and monogamy. It is based on the conviction that human beings are in control of their sexuality, not vice-versa.

Leprosy is the nearest biblical equivalent of AIDS. Jesus touched the leper! It incensed the religious straights; it encouraged the lepers; it inspired the rest.

But Jesus didn't touch him in order to catch leprosy. He didn't touch him in order to bring him, *infected,* back into society, either. He touched him in order to heal him. There's no indication that being a Christian means volunteering for a disease.

So the Christian strategy has to be one of compassion for the victim on the one hand (whether he be "bystander" or "collaborator") and tough-minded realism on the other.

It is nonsense to expect the uninfected public to volunteer for the disease. It is nonsense to allow sexual promiscuity to reduce the national war on AIDS to condom distribution and safe sex seminars. (Although they are better than nothing.)

It is realistic to identify the carrier—and without Nazi tactics. It is realistic to call our society to sexual morality and fidelity. We are not animals at the mercy of heat cycles. We are people who can use our sexuality as an aid to love and creativity. Finally, it is realistic to accept that decisions must be made before a sizable portion of the population vanishes.

Our survival depends on the cure of two syndromes— one viral and one spiritual. Without the latter, we cannot soon muster the courage to conquer the former

The NAACF

A new high school is opening in our town. The school board has announced that it will be named after a Texas hero who died at the Alamo. The NAACP objects. The hero was a slave owner, and naming the high school after him would insult the black community.

I'm a fan of the NAACP. Their contribution to civil justice and the American conscience is without parallel. And this is not an empty accolade. Their work is not nearly done and should go on.

But speaking of parallels, I'd like to see one alongside the NAACP. I'd call it the NAACF: "The National Association for the Advancement of Confession and Forgiveness."

When something as evil as slavery is buried in a nation's

past, it can never be processed without confession and for-giveness. I can never do enough to atone for the sins of my fathers. All I can do is confess them and make sure they're not repeated under my watch.

On the other hand, I can never avenge the wrongs done to my fathers by holding the children of their oppressors responsible. I can demand that they and I not continue to enjoy and suffer the inequities that result from those wrongs. That's the NAACP's task, and it's a worthy one. But ultimately, if we're going to have community, there must be forgiveness. At some point the past must be past. We simply cannot go far enough back into history to right all of its wrongs.

Our country is as racially divided as ever. Racism is a cancer eating at our vitals. I drive by integrated schools and see black children gathered on one side of the school yard and white children on the other. Most of them have been bused from miles away just so they can come to school and remain separate.

We're afraid to tell the truth about the situation. There are lies we let lie because we haven't the national will to face them. For example, we haven't the courage to admit that "counting people by color" is racist whether it's done forcibly to exclude them or to include them. Nor do we have the courage to admit that racism is not peculiar to color. I've been in most parts of the world and I haven't found one place that is free of racism.

White, black, brown, yellow—these are only different hues within the same family called human. Racism is a human phenomenon. It's part of our nature, not our color.

The blockbuster news of 1988 was that every human liv-ing on this planet today is descended from one woman who lived in Africa or Asia about 300,000 years ago. The geneticists say they have proved it. It's a fact.

The implications of this discovery should be enormous. For one thing, there are no races within the human race. The ancient hominids that walked upright millions of years ago died out. They were not "branches" on the human tree.

Most important is this: Every biological difference that exists between peoples of the earth today is the result of a very recent evolution. The human race is biologically one family. But the discovery won't matter much if it doesn't find its way to a spiritual reunion of the human race. And the only way for that to happen is through forgiveness.

The people we've sinned against are *our people!* The people who have sinned against us are *our people!*

Recently I was invited to be "roasted" at a benefit to raise money for a Roman Catholic charity. I considered it an honor. I mean, a Baptist preacher raising money for Catholics!

After the fun at my expense, it was my turn. I did some funnies, and then I said, "My mother is here this evening. Her maiden name was Foy. The Foys came to America about three hundred years ago from France." They all looked at Mom with that "Oh, how sweet!" smile.

Then I said, "Most of the Foys didn't come to America. They were murdered in their beds by Roman Catholics because they were Huguenots. Only a few escaped. My ancestor Foy was an infant saved by his eight-year-old sister who saw her parents and siblings slaughtered."

The place was deathly quiet. Then I said, "I'm here tonight to make a statement." The Monsignor who had invited me was ashen. "Those days are past and best forgotten. Our being here this evening is a testimony to God's intention to eventually make us all one human family." There was an audible sigh of relief just before the applause.

We need civil rights movements and activists and laws. *We don't need civil rights leaders who continue to remind us of the evils of the past in order to maintain their prestige and power.*

The acid test of the true peacemaker is that he works himself right out of a job. We need an NAACF whose main goal is to be so successful that it has to disband.

Everything I've said here could apply to the worldwide Jewish community as well. We need to be reminded of what Hitler did. Indeed, we must never forget. But if the world is to become one there must be Holocaust forgiveness alongside Holocaust remembrance.

We must have the courage to expose the lies we let lie.

Dare It Be Said?

It seems queer, but in this day of verbal glut there are still some unmentionables. I don't know if it's a conspiracy of silence or a lack of nerve, but some things just dare not be said.

For example, it dare not be said that this country's ethical deterioration is primarily linked to the alteration of the traditional family structure for the sake of selfish convenience.

Four institutions are integral to the survival of our system: government, school, church, and family. Oddly enough, the family can survive without any or all of the other three. *But not one of the other three can survive without a strong family unit!*

What is a strong family unit? One that has a mom and dad with mutually accepted roles and lifelong faithful commitments to each other. One that sticks together even when it ain't fun. One that sees discipline as a means to get from "here" to "there." One that gives children boundaries to bump up against. One that has religious and moral values that are higher than immediate convenience. You know what I'm talking about! It's the so-called outdated traditional family.

It dare not be said that the decline of the family is the real culprit in the decline of our culture. Because to say it, we would have to admit that a parent needs to stay home with the baby in its earliest years. We'd have to admit that some people have to fulfill themselves through the fulfillment of others whom they nurture. We dare not say such things in a society where "my freedom" means liberation from responsibility for anyone but the one and only me.

Nor dare it be said that the integration of blacks and whites in this country cannot advance beyond its present sorry estate until all families, *black and white,* are radically strengthened.

Over 60 percent of black children are born out of wedlock. Seventy-five percent grow up in a matriarchal family. Eighty percent of the violent crimes committed in the United States are by blacks, mostly against each other.

White families are self-destructing on the altar of materialistic comfort. Latchkey America is testimony to what parents will pay for two cars, three baths, and tract homes.

The churches of America, black and white, hold out the best hope of calling the nation homeward if they have the guts for battle. Dare it be said, that so far they have not?

The whole truth about American foreign policy dare not be said, either. It dare not be said that we are "selectively righteous." We remain concerned about human rights in

Haiti while turning our backs on Bosnia.

Dare it be said that South Africa was only one of several villains? Dare it be said that we need a convenient villain to hide our own sins? And dare it be said that tyranny is not peculiar to any color? And what about the Middle East? Dare it be said there will never be peace as long as we favor Israel? Dare it be said that it is possible to disagree with Israel without being anti-Semitic?

In a word, dare it be said that if we really wanted a righteous foreign policy we would be evenhanded in our scorn as well as our praise? And dare it be said that in the end all we could find would be regimes who are less evil than others? And dare it be said that there is no such thing as a godly government? Including our own?

Here are a few more dare-it-be-saids: Dare it be said that the Klansman is just as much the product of a demonic system of hatred and ignorance as a ghetto-dweller? Dare it be said that a liberated female is not a woman who succeeds in imitating a man?

Now for the Protestants. Dare it be said that mainline Protestant America has lost its nerve? It is the mouthpiece of the culture's values, not the voice of the culture's conscience. It has sold out. It measures its effectiveness in terms of budgets, political power, and material opulence. It long since gave up trying to transform; now it conforms. No longer can it say, "Gold and silver have I none." Nor can it say, "Rise up and walk."

And dare it be said that even democratic governments like our own form lives of their own which are at enmity with the will of the people and need overthrowing periodically? No one has dared say that since the guys who originally framed our government!

Dare it be said that I have "ripped my britches" by saying all of the above? No doubt! That's why we have so few prophets these days. They've all ripped their britches. They've exposed their backsides. Woe be unto him who does that.

22

THE POWER OF
PRINCIPLE THINKING

Have you seen the television spot that flashes back and forth between the beautiful people who are smoking and laughing at the cocktail party and the emaciated patient who's dying of cancer? It's the one where the voice asks, "Why are these people laughing?"

I ask a similar question about hope. "Why are these people hoping?" Hardly a day passes that we don't hear comments like this: "Everything's going to be okay," or "Things will get better," or "Hang in there."

"Why?" and "Who says?" How do we know things will get better? Why are we incurable optimists? Is it because the alternative is so unbearable, or is there really a reason to hope?

America is hooked on the ideas of upward mobility and inevitable progress. We just know things will get better! We buy products that we know can't live up to their billing. We elect politicians who make us promises that we know they can't keep. We take out thirty-year mortgages without blinking an eye.

What is the basis of our hope? I hope our hope isn't based on our economic system. We don't need to say much about that. One thing will do. In 1987, the two largest exports out of New York harbor were scrap paper and scrap metal. The paper comes back as cardboard containers for

TV sets, computers, and other consumer goods. The metal comes back as Toyotas, Nissans, and so on.

I hope our hope isn't in our political system. Congress, whether of the elephant or donkey variety, has lost its nerve. It bashed South Africa in order to gain the black vote, but shuts its eyes to a hundred other cruel regimes in the world.

For years, the two houses of Congress haven't had the nerve to pass laws on abortion, civil rights, or capital punishment. So they've abdicated their responsibility to the one branch of government that is beyond the reach of the people—the Supreme Court.

And that's the real reason they didn't want a man like Robert Bork on the court. He would have placed the responsibility for drafting laws back where the constitution says it belongs!

I hope our hope isn't in our military power. The world has become too small for military solutions.

Where is my hope? Naturally, you'd expect me to say, "In God." But let me explain. I am a Christian humanist, in case you haven't noticed up to now. I believe that God will always raise up people who are radical enough to believe in the power of Christ to redeem and remake the human spirit. My hope is not in humans left to themselves, but in humans who are related to a God who won't leave us to ourselves.

These are the people who live by what I call the "power of principle thinking." As a youngster I was inspired by Norman Vincent Peale's Positive Thinking. I owe him a great debt, as do millions of others.

As a minister in mid-life, I was inspired by Robert Schuller's Possibility Thinking. It was also a godsend to me.

I started over at forty-three—resigned a church of three thousand members and set up shop in a rented schoolhouse. The church had sixty members and eight hundred dollars in the bank. I had a mortgage, two kids in college, and half a salary.

One year later, I came very close to a heart attack, I had a coronary bypass, and almost died. Four years later we held our first service in a $17 million facility and two thousand people showed up. In the past two years, over three thousand more have joined.

However, I found that there were times when thinking positively didn't create positive results. I also found that all possibilities do not become realities even with faith in God!

I am not criticizing the power of both ways of thinking. I am saying that I discovered principles to fall back on when I ran out of energy to think the other two ways— when I had *positively* lost the energy to consider the *possibilities.*

This may be splitting hairs, but I really believe that it is not a positive mental attitude that gets us through. It is the convictions—I call them "principles"—that lie beneath the attitude. In other words, attitude is a result, not a cause.

I have seen many people go to a motivational seminar and return with the buzzwords and body language of the "positive mental attitude cult": things will get better by the sheer force of our believing they will. Such people believe that a new attitude can be created and sustained cosmetically.

For a while, it can: After all, anybody who exchanges a frown for a smile, lethargy for enthusiasm, and aimlessness for purpose, is going to "win friends and influence people."

But eventually the principles by which that person lives will win out. And when the roof falls in, they are what we fall back on. I don't think Peale or Schuller would disagree with this. I think I'm simply building on what they have said: At any rate, I want to list the principles that form the foundation of real hope.

Wait To Worry

I first learned the "wait-to-worry" principle from Fred Smith, Christian businessman and human extraordinaire. He has the lowest anxiety level I've seen. When I asked how he lived so worry-free, he said, "I really don't know how or when, but God put a neon light inside my brain. Whenever a crisis occurs, it starts to flash, 'W-T-W—WAIT TO WORRY.'"

That was the end of it. Fred seldom explains himself. I started thinking about it. *What if I worried only when it was time to worry?* It would knock a big hole in my worry-time. Then I realized that wait to worry was Jesus' policy. He made it clear in Matthew 6:25-34.

Jesus doesn't say, "Don't worry!" He accepts the fact that to worry is human. We're the only known creatures who can anticipate danger in the future and punishment for the past. So, we can't help but worry.

He does say, though, that we should wait until the proper time and then worry. And He gives us four times to start worrying:

1. *Worry when it will feed and clothe you.* Birds don't farm. Lillies don't weave. Yet they're fed and clothed. They work, but they don't worry. (The reason there's so much worry in America is that more people worry than work.)

During my several trips to the remote African bush, I have observed that although the natives spend most of their days seeking what we call the basics for survival, there is no visible anxiety. I asked our camp manager, Jeremiah, why this was. He said, "We have what you call a proverb: 'Worry does not pass through the belly, or warm the back.'"

You can't eat and wear worry! Until you can, wait to worry.

2. *Worry when it will make you live longer and grow taller.* Wait until worry adds quantity and quality to your life, then worry. Everyone I know who's involved in the human sciences says worry diminishes human life. For that matter, everyone I know says it! I have a zipper-shaped scar on my chest that says it!

3. *Worry when you want to know how a pagan feels.* The word "pagan" can mean either a person who is without a god or a person without a reliable god. It doesn't refer to the classic monster who rapes, pillages, and eats raw meat. A pagan is someone who feels that he or she must face fate either without any gracious support "from above" or with a "maybe God"—maybe He'll help and maybe He won't.

Jesus says if you want to know how that feels, worry. At bottom, worry is "unfaith." It is the suspicion that we do not really have a loving Father who's in the fight with us. Worry is the symptom of an absentee God.

4. *Worry when you want tomorrow to be worse than it's already going to be.* One of our classic relief-phrases is, "Don't worry, everything's going to turn out okay." Jesus blows that one to smithereens! He says: "Don't worry, everything's *not* going to be okay. In fact, tomorrow is going to have its full share of troubles" (Matt. 6:34, my translation). Today's worries will only throw more bricks on tomorrow's wagon, and it's already loaded!

Jesus is saying, God has not cut us adrift in this world.

He's in the boat with us. And He waits for us in "tomorrow."

One night my friend of thirty years called. I had enjoyed watching his growing faith and his growing family and his making millions and his giving millions. "I have no one to talk to," he sobbed. "I've lost my fortune, my family, and my integrity. I'll be indicted for tax fraud tomorrow. Rev., my world has come to an end!"

"No, it hasn't," I said quietly. "You're a child of God. You feel too bad for the world to have ended! A chapter has ended. Turn the page. There's more to come."

My favorite "preacher story" is one that probably never happened, but should have. It's the one about the old New England farmer who took his son to the boat to see him off to World War I. Before the boy went up the ramp to board, he and his father faced each other for a moment. They had never been demonstrative in their affection. Neither knew what to say. So they stiffly shook hands. The father whispered, "God be with you." The boy said, "Good-bye, Father."

On board, the boy watched the old man get into his buggy and start homeward. As the buggy topped a hill, the boy realized that there were many things he had wanted to say to his dad that might never be said.

He raced off the ship and up the road, knowing he couldn't reach his father in time, but pressing on anyway. As he crested the hill, he saw his father in the distance. He had already turned the buggy around and was coming back to meet his son at full gallop!

Worry if you don't have a heavenly Father like that. Otherwise, wait.

Miracles Happen in Miracle Territory

What is a miracle? It's when God intervenes to change something or someone. There has to be (1) a changing of directions, a turning from one course to another; (2) God has to be the one who's causing it; and (3) people have to know that He's the one who's causing it. It takes all of the above to make a miracle.

The reason we have a problem with miracles is that they happen only in "miracle territory." We don't put ourselves in the places where miracles occur.

Why should God get involved in doing what we can do for ourselves? Miracles don't happen in the land of self-sufficiency. It's only when we get beyond the limits of what we know we can do that we experience what God can do.

I'm not saying that miracles depend on our faith. That's the most God-awful evil ever invented. I know a dear couple whose baby boy lay dying with cancer. Some "religious folk" announced to them that the boy could be healed if the parents had "enough faith." God help us!

I'm saying that miracles happen whether we see them or not. We have to put ourselves where we can see them for them to be miracles for us.

How do we do that? The same way you dodge a rhino: First you go where rhino's charge; then you get in front of one; then you dodge it.

Where is miracle territory? It's wherever people stop going it alone. Miracles happen where selfish people become disgusted with themselves, and God turns them into generous people. Miracles happen when liars give up, and God turns them into truth-tellers.

Miracles happen when cowards let go, entrust their destiny to God, and embrace death with serenity. Miracles happen when embittered parents entrust their dying child to God and receive the guts to get on with it.

What about "special effects"? You know, when seas are parted, and water is walked on, and axe heads swim? I don't know. Naturally, I'm skeptical. Did you notice that word I just used... "naturally"?

From what I know of nature, I find it hard to believe such reports. They violate "natural law." But what do I know about nature? What is natural law? It's the sum total of what we know about how the world-we-think-we're-looking-at works!

It's plausible to assume that we still have more to learn. We only discover natural laws, we don't make them. And what a miracle the regularity and symmetry of the natural order is! God has intervened in the midst of nothing and brought forth boundaries and predictability. That is miraculous.

How can anyone study these mysteries without awe? It's hard to believe, but the miraculous does not exist for the seeker of self-sufficiency.

My purpose, however, is not to argue for miracles. It is to share my own encounters with the miraculous. I have never heard a voice from heaven or seen God's handwriting on a wall or raised the dead or healed anyone by touching them. But I have no problem believing these stories, because I believe God raised Jesus from the dead. I believe this because I have experienced the Spirit of God in me through living out Christ's life. If I can embrace the Resurrection, the other reports are a piece of cake.

I have seen brave people launch out into miracle territory individually and become new people. I have seen churches risk their futures by committing resources they didn't have to ministries they couldn't do, but *did!*

In the end, you can't convince people who've never ventured into miracle territory. And you don't have to convince those who have. If you want to see a miracle, you have to go where they are.

Every Mountain Is a Foothill

Have you ever noticed how nothing stays won? Every war was supposed to be the last one. Every social program was supposed to be the ultimate solution. Every problem I solve is replaced by a new one.

The hard truth is that every mountain we climb turns out to be merely a foothill. We live with the illusion that we can reach "ultimate peaks," that we can ascend to the pinnacle and then rest...not so.

And especially "not so," in our journey with God. You can't turn bicycle religion into tricycle religion. Biblical religion is of the bicycle variety: You either move forward or you fall over. Every mountain is a foothill. You climb one and look upward to the next.

The problem with God's people, meaning us, is that we're always trying to make mountains out of foothills. We like to climb up and look down, not climb up and look up.

The record of the children of Israel wandering in the desert is a vivid example. They cried for deliverance and the sea was parted. Then they cried again for water and food. Water, quail, and manna were served. They reached the mountain of Sinai and lost their faith again. They could not understand that every mountain was only a foothill.

The same goes for us. It's true for churches. The church I serve is only fifteen years old. For the past two years it has been one of the fastest growing in the country. One of the keys to its growth has been its "on-the-wayness" attitude. Our people put outreach before personal comfort. They refused to settle for the good when they could have the best.

Yet I am amazed at how quickly we have begun to talk about how we got here, and what used to be, and how we outta rest a spell and "consolidate our gains." We have begun to "look downward" on how far we've come instead of upward to how far we have to go.

Every mountain is a foothill in marriages as well. Nothing stays won. A couple either grows together or grows apart.

I am fortunate to be friend to Willie Nelson. I knew him before he got to be "Willie." One night, several years ago, we were sitting in the living room at Darrell Royal's house when he picked and sang a new song he'd written. Later it would become famous. It starts out:

> People are sayin' that time'll take care of people like me.
> And that I'm livin' too fast, and they say I can't last much longer.
> But little they see that their thought of me is my savior.
> And little they know that the beat outta go just a little faster.
> So pick up the tempo just a little and take it on home....[9]

That's gospel! That's biblical religion! There is no stopping place. There are no Christians, but only people who are in the process of *becoming* Christians. There is no security, no final mountain. We need to pick up the tempo. We're not home yet.

Every mountain is a foothill. People who stop remembering that stop being of much use to God.

It's: "What Happens to What Happens to You!"

For me, the first principle of coping is: *It's what happens to what happens to you.* Contrary to popular opinion, we have little control over what "happens" to us. We can't choose when and where we were born, or our genetic gifts—color, aptitude, economic stratum, susceptibility to disease, or tragedy!

The only real freedom we have is the freedom to choose how to respond—to determine what happens to what happens to us. That's the meaning of human freedom.

In the Book of Philippians, Paul says that he's learned a "great secret" so that he is content in any kind of circumstance (Phil. 4:11–12). He says he's been rich and poor, with and without, comfortable and miserable. No matter. He has learned to determine what happens to what happens to him. Remember, he wrote this from prison. And he says that this secret power of contentment comes "through Christ," but he doesn't explain how.

How did Christ give him the power to choose "what happened to what happened"? I think you have to look at the whole process of Paul's life to find the answer. Four stages in Paul's development brought him to a place where he was free to choose his contentment—to choose "what happened to what happened." These four steps are as valid for us as for him.

Step 1: Confrontation

First, there was *confrontation*. Paul was of the elite ruling class. He was a scholar, a Benjaminite, a protector of religious orthodoxy, an inquisitor.

While in hot pursuit of the Christian cult, he was confronted first by the risen Christ and then by himself. Years later, whenever pressed to explain his life and style, he harked back to the confrontation on Damascus road.

There Christ asked, "Why, Paul?" "Why are you so consumed with doing violence to me and mine?" And then Paul asked himself, "Why?" "Why am I here? Where am I going? For what purpose was I born? Is there any ultimate meaning to my life or to life itself?"

The first key to the secret of contentment is confrontation. Until we confront ourselves and are confronted by a God who is present and accounted for, we cannot respond, we can only react to what happens to us. Without a God "beneath it all" and without a sense that we have a future that counts, we are trapped.

This is really the message of Dickens's famous Christmas story. Tiny Tim, and goodwill, and foodstuffs are the trimmings. The key is Scrooge's transformation. And the key to his transformation is confrontation. When he confronts and is confronted by his death, he becomes "free" to respond.

Prior to this he can only react. Selfishness, grumpiness, anger, bully-tactics—these are the reactions of fear. Giving, pleasantness, warmth, and affection—these are the responses of confrontation.

Step 2: Contemplation

Paul went from confrontation to *contemplation.* He didn't acquire a tent right after he met God and hit the evangelism trail. He went to the desert for three years to sort it all out. It was there that Paul learned the second great key to coping. He learned to live from the inside out. He let what came to him from the inside shape what came on him from the outside.

Not so in our society. Life is lived mostly in reverse— from the outside in. We get up, wash, eat, and go see what will hit us today. If it's pleasant, we have a good day. If it's unpleasant, we have a bad day.

Most of my morning prayers reflect this slavish existence. I begin the day by asking God to let good things happen. What a patsy! I'm guaranteed to lose nine days out of ten. Even if good things happen, they are blurred by the bad.

Contemplation is different. It's asking God for the guts to get through everything that happens. It's the sharpening of our wits—not to outsmart the enemy but to turn him into a friend.

The inward life—meditation, devotion, prayer, study— is not an end in itself, as we shall see, but without it we are like a little fishing cork. We bob to the whims of all the outside forces: the people who pull our strings, the winds and waves, the silently swimming fishes we call "feelings," which jerk us under.

There is no freedom until we acquire the power to choose how we respond to the outside forces. And this power requires an inward eye. Most of us let the outside forces tell us who we are because we haven't spent enough time with ourselves to know ourselves.

Step 3: Participation

Paul determined what happened to what happened to him because he moved beyond confrontation and contemplation. He didn't become a cloistered guru whom pilgrims could go and see by appointment. The next stage was not fixation but *participation.*

He jumped into the thick of it. Paul seldom plowed the same field twice. He never stopped learning and becoming. Up to his dying day at the executioner's block he was planning another missionary journey to another uncharted territory.

In a prison letter, he said he had not achieved "sainthood" but kept striving toward the mark. In another letter, he said he saw the things of God only through a "glass darkly."

People who respond are people who never fixate. Once you fixate—become a settler, fence off your territory, put down roots—all you can do is react to that which threatens your security. If you know who God is (confrontation), and you know who you are (contemplation), you have the energy to dive into history (participation) without fear. You can control what happens to what happens to you.

Step 4: Anticipation

The fourth stage of Paul's contentment was *anticipation.* The future was utterly friendly to him. He had complete confidence in what was to come.

Earlier in Philippians, he says it's really a blessing for him to be in prison. For one thing, some of the prison guards have been exposed to the Gospel. For another, several young Christians have started preaching because he's out of circulation. Some are preaching out of impure motives, but Christ is being preached, and that's what counts (Phil 1:12–20).

And when it comes to dying, Paul says it's okay with him either to live a while longer or to die now. To live is to be with Christ; and to die is even better!

There is no way to respond instead of react, unless we believe there is "more to come." If we have to race the clock and crowd all of the living we can into a brief existence, we can only live with regretful memories and unfulfilled longings—"if onlys" and "what ifs."

Viktor Frankl, the great Jewish psychiatrist who survived Auschwitz, found that the biblical view of freedom we've been discussing was confirmed time and time again by death-camp inmates. Their ability to survive their horrid circumstance was based upon what happened to what happened to them—how they chose to respond, not what was done to them.

"Everything can be taken from a man but one thing," says Frankl, "the last of the human freedoms—to choose one's attitude in any given set of circumstances."

But then Frankl tells us where the power to choose this attitude comes from: "The prisoner who had lost faith in the future—his future—was doomed. With his loss of belief in the future, he also lost his spiritual hold. He let himself decline and became subject to mental and physical decay."[10]

What's going to happen to you?

This isn't the important question. Instead, the important question is, *"What happens* to what happens to you?" And that will be determined by confrontation with who we are and who God is, by our inward contemplative life, by our participation in the unfolding of God's world, and by our anticipation of the future as friend.

There's a "Yes" in Every Mess

"Tough times never last, but tough people do." Right! But what makes people tough? Why do some conquer while others cave in?

I say because of a set of principles—convictions chiseled in the bedrock of the soul by the grace of God. Many of us don't ever know where or when we received them.

One principle that has come to me only after many years is this: "There's a 'yes' in every mess."

There's one sentence in the Book of 2 Corinthians that always jumps off the page at me: "Jesus Christ, the Son of God, is not 'yes' and 'no'... He is God's 'yes'... the 'yes' to all of God's promises" (2 Cor. 1:19-20, my translation).

The church to whom these words were addressed was a mess. Factions, fights, and falsehoods, adultery admired, and orgies at communion. The old man who wrote them had made a mess of his life according to the world's standards. But his words survive as a monument to God's standards.

There is no such thing as a totally negative event or experience. There can be no negative without a positive. There's always a yes buried somewhere in the mess.

There's a yes in every failure. Thomas Edison, who was bounced from school because his teachers branded him "unteachable," spent his time tinkering. After great success, he attacked the challenge of inventing the electric light. Over seven hundred experiments failed. His chief assistant called it quits. "We've failed," he said. "We're not progress-ing." "Nonsense!" said Edison. "We now know seven hun-dred things that won't work!"

And George Fredrick Handel first heard the "Hallelujah Chorus" in his head while paralyzed by a stroke and hiding from his creditors.

The turning point of my life came out of failure. I want-ed my father's blessing, but the only time it seemed attain-able was when I carried a football. So my life's dream became a scholarship to play in the Southwest Conference.

At 140 pounds, I signed and played—for a little while. Then followed a fractured skull, two knees and two shoul-ders out of commission, and a lot of talk about how good I could have been.

At the age of twenty, I had a pregnant wife, several use-less credits, and no place to go.

The yes in the mess was the one and only good lesson to be learned from athletics—how to lose and live through it. You can learn teamwork and discipline in other places. You can experience the thrill of victory and the agony of defeat in other places. You can acquire mental toughness in other places.

But the best lesson you'll learn from sports is how to lose and live over it. Because sooner or later, you'll lose.

It was only because I'd learned to lose and live over it on the field that I had the gumption to search for a new dream.

There's a yes in every failure. There's a yes in every tragedy, too—those caused by people and those caused by "nature." There's no such thing as a senseless tragedy.

Now hold on! I'm not suggesting that God was a reason for them, nor that they make sense. I'm saying there's no tragedy that can't be used for a positive purpose.

One day I arrived at the hospital and found my pal Dick in the emergency room. His son, Rick, was brain dead. The lead doctor for the organ-harvest team came in.

"Yes," Rick's body still functioned. "Yes," there were recipients waiting—eyes for a blind girl, kidneys for a father of two, and the heart for a teenager in Georgia. "No," Rick's body would not cease functioning until the heart was harvested. He was dead, but he wasn't dead.

With his mouth set, with almost grim defiance, Dick said, "Well, Pastor, you say there's a yes in every mess? This is about the only one I can find. Rick can live through others."

Even in bad career choices there's always a yes. I knew it was time to leave a pastorate I once held. I had prayed about it and visited with my closest confidants.

I took the first offer that became available. It was a mistake. Two weeks after I arrived, I knew it was all wrong. But I held on for seven years. I had a family to feed, but mostly I had an ego to support. I couldn't admit accepting a "call" that God didn't issue.

Two great yeses came out of this mess. My son survived premature birth and critical illness because he was born in a city with medical facilities superior to those of the town I had left. And I was given the mission of my life in the founding of a great church. Mistakes cannot be undone, but they can be redeemed. There is always a yes even in the mess of our separation from the will of God. If I may be so bold, there's a yes even in our sins!

However, lest I sound like a cheerleader at a Get-Rich-with-Jesus Seminar, let me emphasize that Paul says the yes in all of our messes is Jesus Christ the Son of God.

"He is God's 'yes'" (2 Cor. 1:19). When I say there's a yes in every mess, I'm not recommending a positive thinking exercise where we always look for the silver lining. I'm saying that because God became one of us and took on all the suffering and won, there is no mess that cannot be redeemed.

There's a yes in every mess because God is in every mess in the person of Jesus Christ! There are some messes so foul that we would probably never find a yes in them. But God is in them, working. That's what Romans 8:28 really says. "God is in all things, *working!*"

On a summer afternoon, a mother put her toddler to sleep in the upstairs bedroom. She left the window open to catch the breeze. The toddler managed to crawl out and fall, impaling himself on the picket fence below.

Carlyle Marney, a great Southern preacher, went to the house. For a long time they sat in silence. The mother asked, "Where is God now?" Marney took a long time, and then said, "I suppose the same place as when His Son was impaled upon a stake."

Ultimately, the only sound reason we have for believing in the yeses is Jesus Christ. If He wasn't and if He didn't and if He can't, then *No* is written across all of reality.

Oh, But You *Can* Begin Again!

Every New Year's Sunday I preach the same sermon. It's pure corn, but equally nutritious! My people know it's coming, and they fill up the place anyway.

I begin with a rebuttal to the old saw that says, "People never change...you can't change human nature." I point out that of all things pertaining to "nature," the human part of it is the most unpredictable and change*able.*

The rotation of planets and atoms don't change. The force of gravity is redundant. But people change all the time. They make new beginnings.

So in typical set-up-the-bad-guys-and-knock-'em-down fashion, I proclaim, "Oh, but you *can* begin again!" The entire biblical drama is one of new beginnings.

After Broken Relationships

The Bible says you can begin again after broken relationships. Nothing hurts worse than the loss of intimacy with a significant other. It's as if the world has ended. But you can begin again.

Ever read the twenty-eighth book of the Old Testament? Hosea is its name. The writer was a prophet whose wife left him and became a prostitute. Out of the depths of his hurt, God told him something like this: "Now you know how I feel. The ones I love keep on becoming whores, too. They sell themselves to other gods. But I keep on buying them back."

Hosea goes and pays to redeem his wife. He feels the same way about Gomer as God feels about Israel: "How can I give you up? How can I abandon you?...My heart will not let me do it! My love for you is too strong." (Hosea 11:8, my translation.)

I don't recommend adultery as a cure for a stale marriage. It's like curing a headache with a bullet to the brain. Yet, adultery doesn't have to spell the end of a marriage. I have seen marriages become stronger after betrayal and healing and forgiveness.

When your mate dies, you can begin again. The same

goes for broken friendships, and divorce, and estrangements between parents and children. Where intimacy is concerned, there is never *the end.*

After Moral Failure

You can begin again after moral failure...after you've done the very thing you said you'd never do...after you've compromised the last shred of your integrity.

Ever read in the Bible about David's moral wreck? I call it Bathshebagate. It involved hanky-panky, adultery, and even the murder of Bathsheba's husband. The postman rang twice, and his name was Nathan the prophet. David was exposed. His past righteousness and achievement were nullified.

But now read Psalm 51. David did the only thing you can do when your caught red-handed. He confessed and asked for a new heart to replace the old one...a spiritual and moral transplant.

Bathsheba was pregnant. She lost the baby. But out of the ashes of this moral collapse, another son was born. His name was Solomon.

Confession isn't a requirement for God's forgiveness. It's the route to it. You can begin again after moral failure.

After Shattered Dreams

You can begin again after shattered dreams...after your great goal eludes you...after you miss the golden ring you've reached for.

Ever read about Elijah? His dream was to call his countrymen back to God. They had gone off chasing the pagan god Baal. The queen, Jezebel, had set up Baal prophets in the court.

Elijah challenged them to a duel at the altars of Mount Carmel and won. The people rallied, overturned the icons of Baal, and slew his prophets.

But in two days the revival was over. In fact, it turned out to have been a lynching instead of a revival. Jezebel's forces were scouring the countryside for Elijah.

He hid in a cave and asked to die. But God told him to get out of the cave and go about his business, and assured him he wasn't the only one who was faithful.

You can begin again after shattered dreams. Look at the chronology of Abraham Lincoln's life:

- 1832　Lost job and defeated for legislature
- 1833　Failed in business
- 1834　Elected to legislature
- 1835　Sweetheart died
- 1836　Had a nervous breakdown
- 1838　Defeated for speaker
- 1843　Defeated for nomination to Congress
- 1846　Elected to Congress
- 1848　Lost renomination
- 1849　Rejected for land officer
- 1854　Defeated for Senate
- 1856　Defeated for nomination to vice presidency
- 1858　Again defeated for Senate
- 1860　Elected president of the United States

Just as there is no such thing as a totally self-made person, there is no such thing as a totally self-ruined person.

I hope I can get away with this one: An Italian immigrant landed in New York in the heart of the Great Depression. He had no skills and was illiterate. Roaming the streets in search of any job, he called at a house of ill-repute. He asked the madam for a job. She said she had need of a bookkeeper, but he couldn't read or write. Out of pity, she gave him fifty cents and sent him away.

He met a man selling bananas. "How much for five bananas?" he asked. "Three cents." "How much for the whole cart?" "Fifty cents." He bought the bundle, divided it, and sold the lot for $1.50.

Thirty years later and still unable to read or write, he owned a chain of supermarkets, which he agreed to sell to a conglomerate for $30 million. At the closing table he signed the sales document with his customary mark, "X."

The lawyer representing the purchaser was amazed. "You mean to tell me that you can't even write your name!" "That's right, but the signature is valid." The lawyer said, "Oh, I don't doubt that it is. But can you imagine what you might have accomplished in your life had you had a proper education!"

"Yeah," the man said. "I would have been a bookkeeper in a whorehouse."

You can begin again! But I shouldn't just leave it there. What does it take to begin again? Two things. An inward revolution and an outward renovation.

You must start on the inside. I'm talking about the "inside-out business" again. Change comes from within. The writer of 2 Chronicles gives a capsule description of this kind of change.

Solomon has finished and dedicated the Temple. He goes home to sleep and God speaks to him in a dream. "This is a high moment," he says. "But in the future when the fervor wanes and the people forget the promises they've made, and bad times set in, tell them: If they will humble themselves and pray and seek my face and turn from the way they are doing life, I will hear from heaven, forgive their sins, and heal their land" (2 Chron. 7:14).

To humble oneself, and pray, and seek God's face is to undergo an inward revolution. To turn from the way you're doing life and toward the way God shows you to do life is to undergo an outward revolution.

But how do you turn? Several years ago I found myself exhausted from unkept promises to God, myself, and my family. I had to alter the way I did my life. It just wasn't working.

So on New Year's Day I listed my priorities:

Time with God; time with family; time with self; and time doing something to make the world a better place (from which I hoped to earn enough money to meet the physical needs of me and mine).

Then I took out the New Year's calendar and tried to translate these priorities into "day-date-time." Ten percent of a week's waking hours is 11.2 hours. That's one hour and thirty-six minutes a day with God.

Time with family meant thirty minutes a day in meaningful conversation with my wife and thirty minutes with my son. It meant a date one night per week with Lois, and at least one overnight trip for just the two of us once a month.

It meant one day a week reserved for my son. It meant writing or calling my "soulmate" friends, parents, and siblings at least once a month.

Time with myself meant recreation, exercise, rest, feeding my mind with good books, and pursuing my hobbies.

I "calendarized" all of this for one month and realized I was in big trouble. You know what happened. I had been lying to myself. "Priority number four" was really "Priority number one." There was no way to maintain my lifestyle, fulfill my ministerial duties, leap tall buildings, do TV, radio, and columns, and leave priority four at four.

Unless... unless I wanted to risk it all. I am trying.

This I know. You can begin again, but it will cost you dearly. Only God can give you that kind of guts. If you haven't the nerve, join the crowd! I'm still trying to muster the courage myself. But as I have dared inward revolution and out renovation, I have found God and the universe to be friendly.

23

"GOOD-NEWS" PEOPLE

The last thing Jesus said to His disciples was that they were to be "good news" people (Mark 16:15).

We talk a lot about Bad-News people. What are Good-News people? Well, I wrote this rhyme. I call it, "The Limerick I Live By." It's not even remotely a limerick, but indulge me. "The Limerick I Live By," has a better lilt to it than "A Rhyme I Run On."

Anyway, it's posted above my desk in calligraphy and I recite it every day. It ain't Wordsworth, to be sure. But it puts the nuts and bolts of a Christian's real hope in terms I can carry around with me. It also sums up the principles I've been talking about in these pages.

A Good-News person is someone who proves there's:

> No rut so deep you cannot leave it,
> No dream so lost you can't retrieve it,
> No pain so great you can't endure it,
> No sin so bad that God can't cure it.

The Guts to Leave the Ruts

Good-News people prove by the way they live, that there's "no rut so deep you cannot leave it."

I learned to drive in the mud. I grew up in the riverbottoms, and if you drove at all, you drove in the mud. There's only one way to drive in the mud—hold the steering wheel steady, put the pedal to the metal, and the car will follow the ruts of those who went before you. If you leave the ruts you're doomed.

People do life that way—pedal to the metal, no turns, follow the ruts. We do it mentally. I'm not really surprised that the Flat Earth Society still exists. Neil Armstrong dealt it a crippling blow when he filmed earth from the surface of the moon, but it wasn't fatal.

Good-News people have guts to leave ruts. In the Old Testament you can read about a twin son, the second to emerge from the womb, holding his brother's heel. His name was Jacob. They named him "heel-snatcher" for obvious reasons, yet his name came to symbolize his life. He "snatched" everything. First it was his brother's birthright, then his father-in-law's two daughters, cattle, sheep, and goats.

While fleeing from his irate father-in-law, he learned that his long lost and equally irate brother was approaching from the other direction. He spent the night by a little brook "wrestling with an angel," with himself, with his ruts. God touched him, and he got up the next morning with a new name: "Israel," ruling with God. He then went on to be reconciled with his brother.

Anwar Sadat was the Christian diplomat of our time. He realized that the ruts of violence were so deep between Egypt and Israel that only a radical gesture in contrast could break the cycle of hatred. He crossed the sea with an olive branch. There's no rut so deep you cannot leave it.

No Lost Dreams

Good-News people prove there's no dream so lost you can't retrieve it.

You can lose fantasies but not dreams. I had plans to get rich, write a best-seller, hunt and fish worldwide, and be a U. S. Senator by the time I was thirty-five. I also planned to marry, raise kids, be a physician, and "do something to help mankind."

At age fifty, I realize that most of those were fantasies. I lost them. But not my dreams.

Fantasies are your ambitions to make a better place for yourself in the world. Dreams are your ambitions to make the world a better place for everybody.

Good-News people keep retrieving their dreams. They are like Moses alone on the "backside" of the desert. They still stop to look at burning bushes. The fires of their dreams cannot be extinguished, even if they're eighty years old!

No Unendurable Pain

Good-News people prove there's no pain so great you can't endure it.

Pain doesn't need to surprise us. We can expect it. It's unavoidable. But neither does it need to paralyze us. We can take it! We don't have to give in to it. Good-News people don't. They cry and hurt and bleed and grit their teeth and use their pain.

Elizabeth Kubler-Ross says every tragedy presents us with a high choice or a low one. She tells of a mother who watched a shark take her four-year-old daughter. For weeks the mom was catatonic. In the following years, she has come to lead a network that ministers to the parents of over ten thousand children who have died violently. She made the high choice.

Rick Hansen, paralyzed from the waist down at fifteen, wheeled himself around the world in his wheelchair. For what? To raise $10 million for spinal cord research!

Then there was Ron Wakefield, who loved to compete in sports. He had good basic athletic skills, but he was not quite in the "great" category. He was fast, but not a world-class sprinter. He was good in football but too small for college and the pros. He had the heart of a lion and the will of a Puritan.

He kept searching until he found cross-country running. He had the build and the speed for it. And God knows he had the heart and the will. It was made to order for Ron.

He went to a small college and asked the coach for nothing but the opportunity to run. And he did run—to a full scholarship at the school and then to a scholarship in the big-time at the University of Texas.

Then cancer struck. He kept running until he couldn't. So he adjusted his goal. He would graduate before he gave in to the disease. And he did! In cap and gown and wig and pain.

He adjusted his goal again. He would die with dignity. No giving up. No surrender. Hand-to-hand with a foe he knew he couldn't beat. At his funeral we sang, "Joy Comes With the Morning."

Ron was no loser. He "ran the race" all the way to the finish line. He didn't stand on a little box with a gold-plated medal around his neck while they played the national anthem before 100,000 people. He stood with his arm around Christ while the angels sang, "Joy Comes With the Morning." He used his pain to learn more about life in twenty-four years than most of us do in seventy-five.

No Uncurable Sin

Good-News people prove there's no sin so bad that God can't cure it.

My biblical heroes are the ones who fall down and get up and fall down and get up. They are real sinners like David. He slew lions and bears and giants with his slingshot, went from shepherd to king in record time, wrote poetry, did in the bad guys, and was even said to have stolen God's own heart.

Then one night he saw Bathsheba. We all know the story. But when the prophet Nathan confronted David with his sin, he didn't say, "I made an error in judgment." Instead, he openly admitted his sin.

David's masterpiece of confession has survived the centuries in Psalm 51. David knew God could cure his sin and He did—giving David a whole new way of doing life. He and we are Good-News people!

EPILOGUE

IF I HAD ONE SHOT

I didn't want to fire a big shot at one issue when I started this book. I wanted to fire little shots at a lot of issues.

Getting it published was secondary. I wanted to leave something for my grandchildren to read and say, *"That's what he stood for."*

I also wanted to offer a kind of believing and doing for those wonderful folks whom the church used to call "heathen," but now call "secular." I hope whoever reads this will get more of a sense of "Who I am" than of "What I have to say."

Now that I'm done, I'm wondering about a parting shot. If I could publish only one vignette, what would I say?

Tomorrow it would probably be something else. But today it is this: *The good news I've had in these years of wayfaring is that I'm not in charge; and the great news is that I don't have to be.*

For years I preached that we can't save ourselves, but I kept trying to save *myself.* I did all of those guilt-and-gut-grinding things a "good Christian" and a "good Christian minister" was supposed to do.

I ended up hating God for it, and myself as well. I don't understand all of those explanations of how Jesus' death on the cross atoned for my sins, so I won't spend time on what I don't understand. But here's what I do understand. Because Jesus died, I can let go of trying to save myself. I'm already accepted and acceptable.

How did I come to know this? Well, I just did. When I let go of trying to be my own god, I met the One who lives.

Do you know what this says about those of us who are trying to "righteous" ourselves into God's favor? We are idolaters. We worship our own abilities to measure up. We are our own god!

Here's some more "good and great" news: *The good news is I can't save you. And the great news is that I don't have to.* I ain't in charge of that, either!

It's been a big relief to realize that I don't have to measure who I am by how full the church is. What's more, the "eternal condition of your soul before God" ain't none of my business. I have not been assigned to punch your ticket at the Pearly Gate!

A little girl—about six years old I'd say, because she had the two front ones missing—stood at the door and said, "You wanna buy thome tickets to the firemanth's danth?" "When is it?" I asked. "I dunno." "Where is it?" "I dunno." "Do you know who I am?" "Yeth," she said, "You're the Creature from the Church."

"You don't know much about what you're selling," I said. "Look, Misthter. I'm thellin' ticketh. I don't know nothin' about the danth. I'm not goin' mythelf. But if you want thome ticketh, here they are!"

Like that little girl, I don't know much about the Dance. I'm not sure I'm going myself. I don't have to judge you, police you, or protect you. I don't even have to know all of the answers. I just sell tickets.

But the best news I've heard on my journey is that I don't have to save God. You'd think that I would have known that right off. Not so. The biggest of all the heresies is the belief that we can save God from heresies.

Religious beliefs are always human interpretations of experiences with God. This means they are never fixed and final. All religious beliefs are in a sense less than true because they are accommodated to our dim understanding.

It was a high day in my life when I realized that it was okay to doubt and to challenge *any* sacred doctrine. None of the cows are holy in the Kingdom of God. It was also a high day when I realized that I no longer had to correct all of the "wrong" people in the world. God can defend Himself.

I can't save myself, or you, or God. And I don't have to. That's about it up to now. Except for these words from Will Campbell's *Brother to a Dragonfly.* Wish I'd thought of them first.... They're what I believe, too:

> "...tell me what the Christian faith is all about.... Keep it simple. In ten words or less." We were going someplace or coming back from some place when he said, "Let me have it in ten words." I said, "We're all bastards but God loves us anyway." He swung the car off on the shoulder and stopped.... After he'd counted the number of words on his fingers [he said], "I gave you a ten-word limit. If you want to try again, you have two words left." I didn't try again.... [11]

NOTES

[1]M Scott Peck, *The Different Drum* (New York: Simon & Schuster, 1983), p. 297.

[2]Harry Emerson Fosdick, "A Fundamentalist Sermon by a Modernist Preacher," *Twenty Centuries of Great Preaching,* Vol. IX, ed. Clyde Fant & William Pinsen (Waco, TX: Word Books, 1971), p. 41.

[3]Gordon MacDonald, *Restoring Your Spiritual Passion* (Nashville: Oliver Nelson, 1986), pp. 73ff.

[4]John E. Keller, *Let Go, Let God* (Minneapolis: Augsburg Publishing, 1985), pp. 22-27.

[5]Charles S. Mueller, *Thank God I Have a Teenager,* (Minneapolis, Augsburg Press, 1985), p. 66.

[6]Alexander Solzhenitsyn, *Warning to the West* (New York, 1975), Farrar, Straus, Girou, p. 130.

[7]Martin Seligman, "Blues Boomer," *Psychology Today* 22, No. 10 (October 1988), p. 55.

[8]As reported in the *Austin American Statesman,* August 12, 1987.

[9]"Pick Up the Tempo," by Willie Nelson, © 1974, 1976 by Willie Nelson Music Company. International Copyright secured. Made in U.S.A. All Rights reserved.

[10]Viktor Frankl, *Man's Search for Meaning* (New York: Washington Square Press, 1959), pp. 104, 117.

[11]Will D. Campbell, *Brother to a Dragonfly* (New York: Seabury Press, 1977), p. 220.

ABOUT THE AUTHOR

GERALD MANN is a minister, writer, businessman, TV personality, humorist, public speaker, and a voice for common sense Christianity. He has a diversified background and experience in human relations which have enriched his views on life and have made him a very able and sensitive counselor.

Dr. Mann has been featured in *TV Guide, USA Today, Advertising Age,* and *Texas Monthly.* He has been quoted by "NBC Nightly News," Paul Harvey, and nearly every major newspaper in America, including *US News and World Report* and *The Wall Street Journal.* Currently, he is the host of "Common Sense Religion," a live, call-in, national TV program which is seen four times weekly on Faith and Values Network.

Author of several books, including *When the Bad Times Are Over For Good* and *When One Day at a Time Is Too Long,* Mann is a communicator whose universal messages apply to everyday life. He is the senior pastor of Riverbend Baptist Church in Austin, Texas—a church of over four thousand members. He lives with his wife Lois in Austin, and has three children: Cindy, Stacey, and J. J.